W9-CIN-157

# THE HUMAN TOUCH

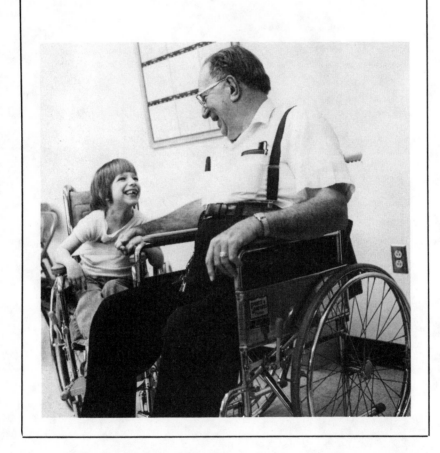

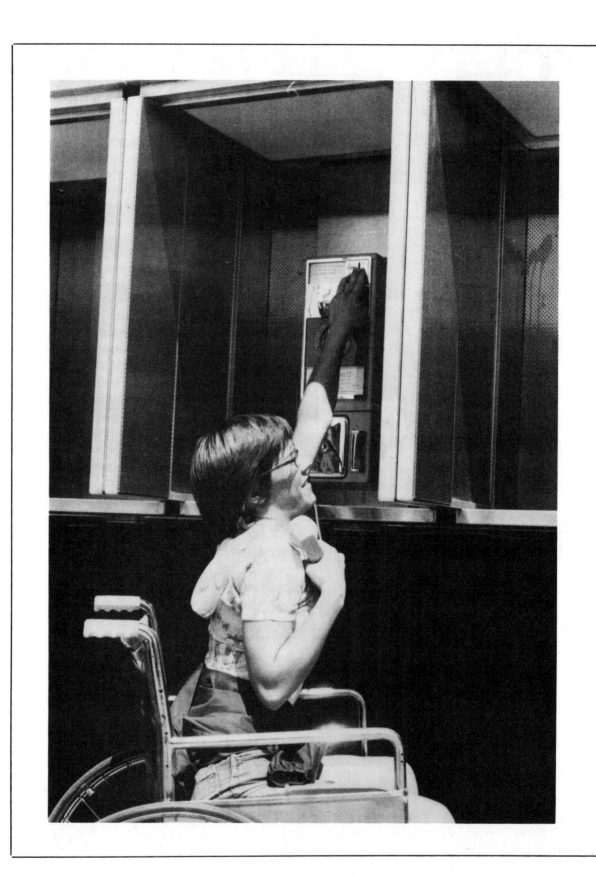

# THE HUMAN TOUCH

## The Story of Easter Seals

## Pat Boone

WIESER & WIESER, INC.
*New York*

Copyright © by Pat Boone, 1991

All rights reserved.

Produced by Wieser & Wieser, Inc.
118 East 25th Street
New York, NY 10010

ISBN 0-914373-22-6

To Edgar "Daddy" Allen and Blanche—
you touch us still today.

*Mrs. Allen (seated left)* and Mrs. Gates (seated right) *whose $25,000 donation made construction of Gates Hospital possible, preside at tea. Daddy Allen stands at far left.*

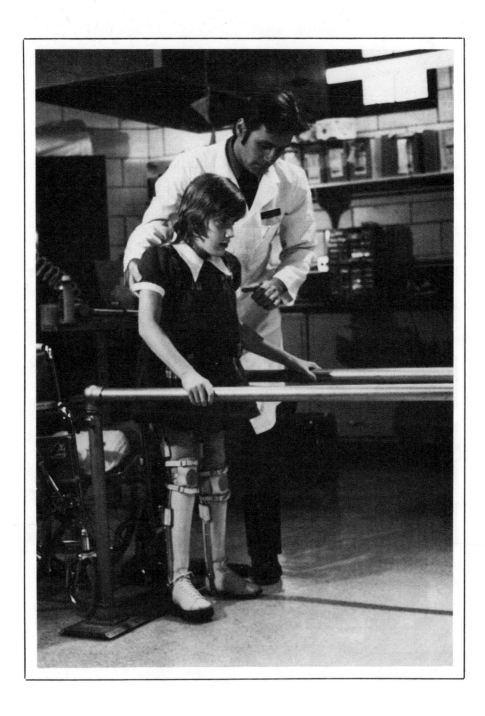

# Contents

# Acknowledgments

On this page I thank everyone who helped as I gathered memories, photos and stories about Easter Seals . . .

Dorothy Burns, her daughter Joan Moore, and Netty Clark for their memories of Gates Hospital in Elyria, Ohio.

Marjorie Fehlner, from the Easter Seal Society of Lorain and Huron Counties in Elyria, Ohio, for her collection of early Easter Seal photographs.

The Elyria, Ohio, Easter Seal Society for early articles about the Easter Seal movement.

The families who have represented Easter Seal programs and services these last ten years:

*Colleen Finn, her parents Jack and Susan and brother John.*

*Mary Sacco, her parents Dan and Anne and brothers Danny and Johnny.*

*Matt Huston, his parents Ron and Carol and sister Jeanne.*

*Stephanie Swiney, her parents Bobby L. and Carla and sister Tre.*

*Danielle (Newman) Sibley and her parents Diane and Trevor Sibley.*

*Jamie Brazzell, his parents Jimmy and Denise and sister Rhiannon.*

*Susie Wilcox, her mother Louise and sister Katie.*

*Shawn Dennstead, his parents Diane and Terry and brother David.*

*Joy Hall, her mother Janet and grandmother Loraine Mitchell.*

*Vanessa Vance, her parents Louis and Vivian and brothers Paul and Jeff.*

*Bridget Houlihan, her parents Tom and Patsy.*

Easter Seal Adult Representatives: Bart van Housen, George Sagona, Andrew Vangelatos, George and Vera Cisneros, Walt Shinault, Kay Stewart, Cyndee Pearson.

Special heartfelt gratitude to Gail Moss, executive editor, who with the staff at the National Easter Seal Society searched through the archives to make this book a reality. They each deserve a medal!

And all the corporate sponsors, these big-hearted men and women—I love you!

# THE HUMAN TOUCH

# Preface

I'm one of those strange people who actually enjoyed history in school. A lot of kids don't, probably because there are so many dates and names to try to remember, and it seems so dry.

"Why should I care about all of that stuff, those wars and dates and events that have so little to do with my world today?" kids have said through the centuries when older people ask them to study history.

I didn't enjoy having to learn dates either, but whenever I could catch a glimpse of the real people who actually lived, I was usually fascinated. My imagination would kick in, and I would start placing myself in their circumstances, and live alongside them as history literally unfolded.

Too often, I think, people associate history with wars, suffering, death and destruction. At best, it's "ages and eras and periods."

But there's another side to history—the one that always interested me—the people and events that contributed to the progress of humanity rather than its tragedies. This other side of history still involves plenty of struggle, but the focus is on accomplishment, rather than destruction and loss. Unfortunately, a lot of the great stories aren't in most of our history books. It's a shame, really, because noble deeds and breakthrough accomplishments are the best way to chronicle man's progress, and they remind us that lots of good things do happen, that people struggling for good usually do win and that historically most things do change for the better.

These are stories that give us strength.

They energize us and encourage us to continue on with our own personal struggles toward our own higher goals.

I'd like to tell you one of those stories now. It's a story that started early in this century, and it's still going on. In fact, it's not even near its final chapter yet.

It's a story that means a great deal to me. It reinforces my belief in the positive side of humanity, the growing and developing side of people, at a time when so many news stories can be quite depressing. It's a story that has involved me for the past ten years. And after you hear it, I think you'll want to be involved in the ongoing saga yourself.

It's the story of Easter Seals.

"Easter Seals?" you say. "There's a story to Easter Seals? Why would that interest me?" Stay with me and you'll find out.

If I remember correctly, I was asking some of those questions myself in 1980 when some Easter Seal executives asked for a meeting with me in my office. I was "clued in" ahead of time that they would be asking me to host the Easter Seal telethon that coming year, and I was not enthusiastic about the idea.

Oh, I'm all for telethons, and certainly had a favorable impression of the Easter Seal efforts, though I had only vague ideas about what those efforts were. It seemed to me that Easter Seals had something to do with infantile paralysis, or birth injury, or some other kinds of diseases, but I wasn't sure. I supposed Easter Seals did something good and commendable, and I knew the organization had been around a long time, but that was about the scope of my knowledge.

I decided to extend the courtesy of meeting with these people, but before we even spoke I had prepared my turndown speech.

At the time I was involved in a number of different charities—world hunger programs, inner-city programs, Bible distribution programs, prison rehabilitation programs—and I had just completed several years as honorary chairman of the National Association for the Blind. I felt I was really too busy to take on anything else.

I also felt that since I asked people for money for all these other charities, it would detract from my effectiveness as a telethon host.

But during our meeting, as the Easter Seal representatives were telling me what the organization was all about, I found myself being more and more impressed.

I hadn't realized Easter Seals was one of the very first and largest voluntary charitable agencies providing services to people with disabilities. Nor had I known it had started back in 1919, had thousands of volunteers and was helping over a million people every year!

I was even more impressed when I learned that over 90 cents of each dollar raised actually stayed in the community where it was raised and went directly into services to people with disabilities in that community.

The Easter Seal people then pointed out that doing a telethon might actually help underscore some of the other causes I was involved in. That touched a sensitive nerve in me. I began to consider agreeing to just one year's commitment, mainly because I was so intrigued with Easter Seals itself.

The more I heard the more I thought, "Gee, this is a great thing. Why don't we know more about what Easter Seals does?"

I thought maybe it was because Easter Seals was so encompassing and so diverse that people couldn't put a handle on it easily. They couldn't associate it with just one disease because it addressed all kinds of problems.

Whatever the disability was, Easter Seals tried to help, and tried to help right within the person's community.

I was impressed. I agreed to do the telethon, but for one year only. They said, "Fine, that's all we're asking." Before they left they gave me some more information—and the more I read about Easter Seals the more impressed I was.

I've now hosted the telethon for ten years.

And since my tenth anniversary with Easter Seals coincides with its 71st year in operation, it seems to me a good time to take a look at how this amazing organization came into being—a tall order!

It's pretty hard to tell the story of something that's operated for so many years and involves thousands and thousands of people in centers all over this nation. It seems almost like that dreaded word "history."

But it's not hard to tell the story of Edgar F. Allen, the man who started the organization that became the National Easter Seal Society. I think anyone might enjoy hearing who he was, what he hoped to achieve and how he reached his goals. And as you find out about him, you'll also learn the story—the many stories—of Easter Seals.

My curiosity about the history of Easter Seals led me to a rough draft of memoirs Allen dictated to his secretary shortly before he died. In them he describes how and why he established an organization to serve people with disabilities. The memoirs are a good demonstration of how to turn dreams into reality. How to make a life count. How to overcome defeat. How to achieve what everyone says is impossible. How to set a force in motion with such momentum that it continues on and thrives even after you've gone.

If you are like me, you wonder sometimes where organizations came from. Why is there an IBM? Who started Xerox? Was there a real General Motors, and how did he start a car company? I hope that reading the story of a kind and gentle man, a man with a desire to help people in his own community, a man with a dream that grew and grew, will interest you.

Edgar "Daddy" Allen and his dream became something far larger than even he could have imagined in the beginning, something larger than he even intended, and it's the real stuff of which history is made. The best kind of history.

As this story unfolds, and as you actually hear from Daddy Allen himself (from quotations from his speeches), as you look at the pictures and get to know the people who have caught and fed the dream and turned it into reality, I think you'll fall in love with Easter Seals.

I think you'll come to appreciate, even revere *the human touch* in all of us, and what it can accomplish.

Pat Boone

*Elyria Memorial Hospital, built after a tragic street car accident in Elyria under the leadership of Daddy Allen.*

# I
# Beginnings: Daddy Allen

*F*rom Edgar Allen's memoirs:

> *I was born, as the records prove, about five o'clock on Thursday morning, May 8, 1862, in what was then the village of Newtonville [Massachusetts]. They used to say I was born early enough for a nice breakfast and perhaps that accounts for the fact that I enjoy breakfast more than any other meal. Perhaps it also accounts for the fact that I was always an early riser.*

Right away, Edgar Allen is a very likable person.

Allen's grandfather, Phineas Allen, was a Harvard professor who made a point of steering his grandson away from any notions the boy might have of becoming a teacher himself.

"I can speak seven languages and I only earn $50 a month for doing it" was the statement Phineas often made to little Edgar (as a fellow who started out to be a teacher myself, I surely empathize and identify with old Phineas' advice, though I deplore the situation he describes).

Edgar got his message, and resolved as a young man to pursue a career in business rather than education. Actually this decision showed some pluck because Allen's father,

Horatio, was not a notable success himself.

> *My father was a school teacher and graduated from that business into the insurance business and did quite well during the Boston fire. During the panic of 1873–76 however he seemed to have lost everything he had gained and later we were obliged to give up our home and finally moved to Cleveland where we had an uncle who had secured a position for my father as a teacher at Linndale.*

Despite the difficult times his family faced, Allen's desire to be a man of business remained undaunted. He trusted his own business sense and felt confident in his ability to succeed.

He was in his teens when his family moved to Ohio, where he quickly found a job as a clerk in a Cleveland hardware store. While working there he married Blanche Wood of New London, Ohio, on the same day in 1886 that Grover Cleveland married Frances Folsom—as Allen was fond of pointing out. Allen and his wife had two sons, Frank and Homer.

As a young man Allen made friends with local businessmen and assiduously studied the newspapers to get a sense of where business was heading and what trends were developing in this growing nation.

He knew that the railroad and telephone industries were expanding rapidly, and perceived there would be tremendous demand for railroad ties and telephone poles—all made from cedar logs. Allen persuaded several friends to back him and at the age of 27, in 1889, he started his own business as a buyer and seller of cedar logs.

*It seems to me as I think it over I was never particularly dissatisfied, but always unsatisfied with my position and so when the opportunity came, as it did in 1889, to form in the city of Cleveland what was later known as the Cleveland Cedar Company, by friends of mine who were able to contribute a little capital, they sent me into the woods of northern Canada to start buying cedar for railroad ties and telephone poles which were in great demand.*

*So in the middle of December in 1889 I left for the North. I knew nothing about cedar, in fact I didn't know a cedar tree when I saw one, but I accumulated a little knowledge as well as quite a fine friendship with the rugged natives of the Indian Peninsula in Ontario, Canada. This offered an opportunity to develop the very thing we were after and we were able to buy, under favorable conditions, quantities of cedar.*

Shortly after the company opened, Allen signed a major contract to supply poles to another young and growing concern—the A. T. & T. Company. His memoirs recount the moment when he got the contract that launched his company:

*. . . after a few pleasantries, I was asked this question: "Supposing we decided to give you the entire contract, what would you do?" With a composure I didn't feel, I answered, "I would hold on to the chair and control myself as best I could and would assure you you had made no mistake!"*

The venture was an enormous success, and Allen became a wealthy man. The Edgar Allen story could end right here, and for many other fortunate men it might have. But his was just starting.

In the years that followed Allen led a pleas-

ant, happy life. He was wealthy, had a nice home, a wife and family and owned an extremely successful business venture. He was a leading figure in Elyria, Ohio, and was a member of the Chamber of Commerce.

But then tragedy struck. His son Homer, then 18, was killed in a streetcar accident. Here's Allen's account of this event:

*There happened to be a great street car accident in . . . Elyria on Decoration Day evening in 1907 . . . The car stopped at Sixth Street. In back of it was coming a large express car which did not stop but jammed into it, killing 16 and injuring 68.*

*There were no facilities in Elyria for caring for such a catastrophe. There was a little private hospital on West Avenue where they were rushed. No beds to take care of them, at least far from enough.*

*When they had gotten in touch with Mother and myself, we found Homer [our son] not in a bed but on the floor and the injuries were such that in connection with the shock he lived only about five hours. . . .*

*A few days after the funeral of my boy I was invited to the Chamber of Commerce to meet quite a representative number of citizens in connection with planning for a new hospital.*

*I had spent up to that time all my life with the thought of two things: business success and money making, and my own family.*

*This was the turning point of my life. I sold out my business.*

*Two weeks after this particular incident . . . I had raised $105,000 to build the hospital. Ground was broken in September, 1907, and the cornerstone laid in November of the same year. It opened Oct. 30, 1908.*

Allen was offered the presidency of the hospital but chose instead to be its treasurer and executive committee chairman, positions he occupied for many years, always without pay.

After his son's death, Allen pursued a very different kind of life. He abruptly left the world of the entrepreneur and entered the world of philanthropy and charitable works—and he never looked back.

But the traits inside the man remained the same. Whatever Allen did, he was energetic,

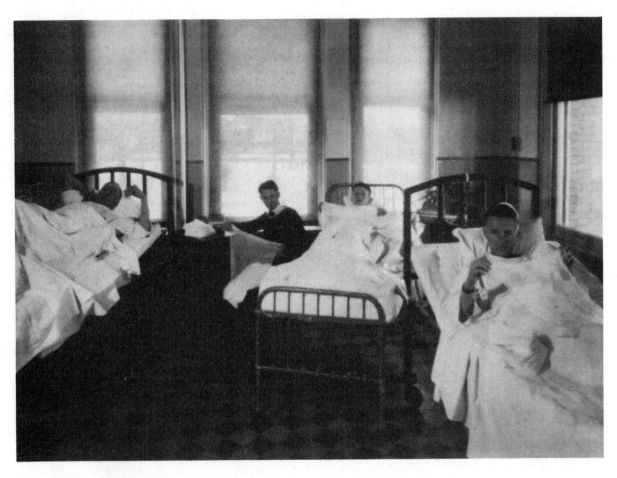

*A boys' ward at Gates Hospital.*

hard-working, dogged, perceptive and de-voted to action. The character and vision that had brought him such success in the business world served him in a completely different way.

In just over a year after Homer's death, Allen had managed to get the hospital built that, had it existed before, might have saved his son's life. He had seen a need, and taken action to meet that need.

It didn't take long before he saw another need that would occupy him for the rest of his life. His response to that need would even-tually result in the National Easter Seal Society.

# A New Focus

In Daddy's memoirs is the story of Jimmie Bodak:

*In the fall of 1909 Dr. H.D. Baldwin, a member*

*of the surgical staff of the Elyria Memorial Hospital, brought in a little boy from Lorain—James Bodak, a cripple, to see if something couldn't be done for him. He was about eight years old and badly doubled up.*

17

*I became particularly interested in little Jimmie because he was bright and clever.*

*That interest in Jimmie in connection with a discussion with the doctor started the crippled children movement.*

*I remember very distinctly what Dr. Baldwin said to me. "You got the hospital built, and got it going, now here is a little crippled child. Why don't you do something for crippled children?"*

*I asked him where the crippled children were and what could we do. He replied, "We don't know how many there are; we don't see them, but there are lots of them."*

*I was very much impressed.*

*So I employed a social worker, Mrs. Van Ostrand, to make a survey . . . of Lorain County . . . to locate these children. . . . At the end of three months she brought a list of 252 crippled children in the county, which after all was not the complete number. But it was astounding to me.*

*We established a ward in the main hospital for children and we used it for crippled children.*

Allen was very much a man of action. When he perceived the potential for a business buying and selling cedar logs, he had acted. When he realized, painfully, that Elyria desperately needed a hospital, he acted. And when a doctor asked him to do something for children with disabilities, he acted.

Allen acted with great energy but also sensibly, methodically. He responded to the doctor's request by conducting a survey to determine the size of the problem. Were there just a handful of children like Jimmie, or hundreds? The survey results astonished him. How could over 250 children with problems like Jimmie's be living in Lorain County if he had never seen them?

Allen developed a fatherly affection for Jimmie, whose physical limitations hadn't diminished his intelligence or charm. And Jimmie, an orphan, had such fond feelings for Allen that he asked if he could call him "Daddy." Allen, of course, agreed, and as time passed, became quite familiarly known as "Daddy" Allen.

He wanted to do something to help Jimmie and children like him. But what? And how?

*A classroom at Gates Hospital.*

18

# Daddy's Mistake

From Allen's memoirs:

*This survey set me thinking. I wanted to find out what was being done and what could be done . . . [and] if the survey in Lorain County was peculiar to itself or whether it was an average set-up for a county.*

*A . . . survey . . . in Huron County and Ashland County showed about the same thing. . . . And a survey of Cleveland . . . found 4,000 cripples, about half of whom were under the age of 16.*

*The next thing was to find out what was being done in the state of Ohio for crippled children.*

*[I soon learned that] Ohio had not spent directly for crippled children $1 in over a hundred years—its period as a state.*

Hard to believe, isn't it? But America was still relatively young, and had been devoting all its energies as a society to building, growing, prospering and realizing the dreams of the fit, the able-bodied, sublimely optimistic. There were some "child work laws," but precious little attention paid otherwise to children. Children were parental responsibilities, after all.

Amazed at the lack of care available for children with disabilities, Allen spent the next three years bringing this problem to the attention of as many people as he could. He started a fund and began raising money to build a hospital for children with disabilities.

After he received a gift of $25,000 from Mrs. W. N. Gates as a memorial to her husband, construction on the hospital began. The W. N. Gates Hospital for Crippled Children, built on land adjacent to Elyria Memorial Hospital, could accommodate 45 children. It was brand spanking new, completely equipped and ready. Allen thought the hospital would fill up immediately. But he was wrong. Almost nobody came. And the hospital stayed nearly empty for months.

*I had gone ahead and built a hospital. I got the money from Mrs. Gates. I don't believe I had really gotten the essence of the problem of the crippled into my heart and head at that time. I was more ambitious for Elyria and the hospital.*

*The hospital hadn't been open very long when we found the crippled children didn't come. Just a few adults came and no one was paying anything for them. I realized we had to start all over again.*

Allen was perplexed. His surveys had located over 700 children with disabilities living in the three counties surrounding Elyria. Wasn't Gates Hospital just what they needed? The man who had stacked up so many successes in his life had now built a hospital that didn't attract any patients. What a stunning, embarrassing puzzle!

At that point, Allen might have left the situation alone. He might have said there wasn't much he could do if people chose not to take advantage of services available to them. I can imagine many practical men, in a comparable situation, saying "Well, if these people haven't got the sense to use the hospital I built them, let them look after their own problems then. I'll go back to business, where my work is appreciated."

But instead he took a deeper look at what he was dealing with. He realized he had tried to solve a problem before he fully understood it, and therefore his remedy, though well-intentioned, had failed to cure. It seemed to have missed the mark completely. He dug deeply into the situation, and found he had erred in several ways.

Allen hadn't known when he built Gates Hospital that parents of children with disabilities commonly distrusted hospitals and surgeons. He learned that the families often hid

*Child and older man, both in wheelchairs.*

20

these children from the public eye, sometimes from shame and embarrassment, sometimes from a desire to protect and shelter the children.

Many of the parents couldn't bear the thought of being separated from their disabled children, who often were favored within the family and rarely allowed to go away from home, especially not to a boarding school or a hospital. The families often didn't want town officials or people doing surveys to even know they had a child with a disability.

Allen knew many of these children could be helped if their families could be persuaded to accept treatment. He needed to find a way to accomplish this. He also knew he needed a more broadly based organization to help him achieve his goal. And he needed a way to offer care for these children that minimized the trauma of physical separation from their parents. Following his usual pattern of observation, analysis and then action, Allen rather quickly found a way to achieve all three of these objectives.

# The Next Step

Allen refused to believe that Gates Hospital was a wasted effort. He remained convinced of the benefits the hospital could provide to disabled children—if only he could get the children to come. He was a man of tremendous perception, with a keen ability to analyze the significance of events—as well as the reasons for their success or failure.

He knew why he hadn't been filling Gates Hospital when he heard about a woman in Sandusky, a nearby town, who was one of the few people actually sending children to Gates. Mrs. Fields, of the Women's Federated Clubs of Sandusky, became interested in children with disabilities after hearing about the survey Allen had conducted there through the efforts of Mrs. Van Nostrand. Mrs. Fields got the names of the children on the list from Mrs. Van Nostrand, but then took Allen's survey one step further. She began visiting the homes of these children and, after establishing a relationship of trust and concern with the parents, told them about Gates Hospital. But her efforts didn't stop there. She also raised money for their care at Gates—initially, $100 per year, and later a dollar a day.

Her process showed Allen where he had gone wrong. He had failed to include the "human touch," as he described it, and he saw that without that touch his plans to help children with disabilities would go nowhere.

Mrs. Fields also demonstrated to Allen that if work with children with disabilities was going to succeed, it ought to take place on the community level. This set his mind racing. Quickly, he reasoned that the only way to get this kind of work done would be through local voluntary organizations. In this way, the families of disabled children would not be dealing with strangers, but with members of their own community interested in offering help.

The mystery of the empty hospital had been solved—and its solution provided the framework for the organization that grew into the National Easter Seal Society—grassroots, community-based assistance to people with disabilities.

Allen now knew he had to approach local organizations with his plan. Surely one or all of them would be just as excited as he was about the potential for helping children with disabilities in their own community. Sadly, and frustratingly, he found that assumption wrong. He was to discover that most local organizations weren't terribly interested—that is, until he went to Rotary with his project.

*Fitting braces at Gates Hospital.*

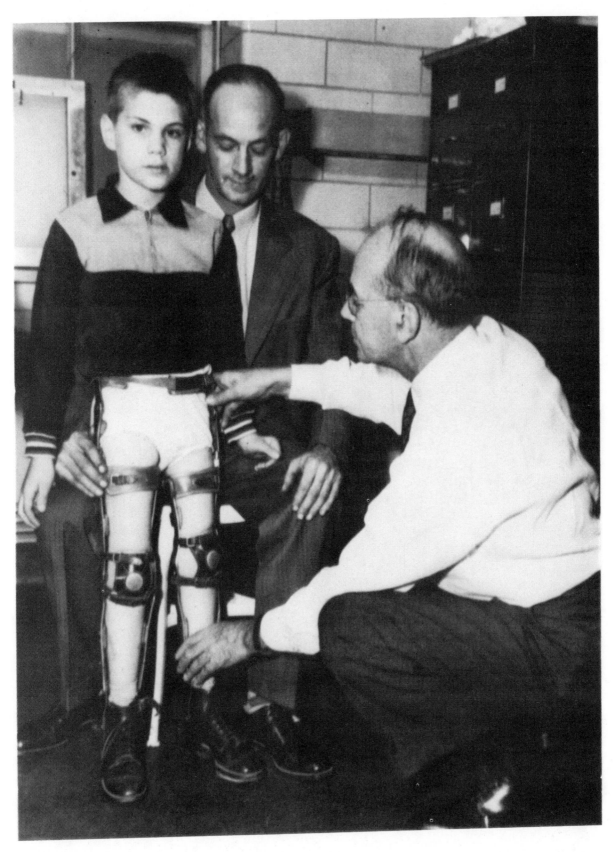

# II
# Rotary Involvement

From Daddy Allen's memoirs:

*I had to get in back of the movement a clientele. I tried the Chamber of Commerce, Y.M.C.A., Women's Clubs, etc., but didn't seem to get very far.*

*Sam Squires at the time was going to start a Rotary Club so in desperation I joined it and hitched my kite for crippled children to Rotary.*

*We went into Rotary in Elyria and the thought in the mind of Sam Squires, president, and Ben Hindman, secretary, was that there would be something to develop as far as the Rotary Club of Elyria was concerned and to translate the slogan of Rotary. "He profits most who serves best" into actual deeds.*

*. . . Crippled children work was something that had not been taken up and that thought in the Elyria Rotary group's mind developed to a point where it was decided to call a meeting. . . .*

*They had asked me to present the entire proposition under the title of "Is It Worthwhile?" . . . and that brought out later in 1918 a meeting of 250 people from Cleveland, Toledo, Sandusky, and Elyria.*

*At the conclusion of the meeting a Resolution was adopted.*

*This became historical in view of the fact that through the influence of Rotary and of the Resolution, it was translated into actual deeds and accomplishments which affected the lives of thousands of children in Ohio and later the development of the entire movement throughout the World.*

*The resolution read:*

*"Let us tonight join hands and start in this old Buckeye State a movement which shall not stop until every unfortunate little crippled child in the State has had its chance to run and play and enjoy God's beautiful world in which it lives. Surely such a task is worthy of Rotary and he who would not aid in its accomplishment is not worthy to be a Rotarian."*

*It was through Rotary that the nucleus of most Societies was formed. Ohio Plan [which focused on community-based facilities rather than a centralized hospital] was used.*

*I might say immediately after that we organized the Ohio Society for Crippled Children which was to be made up of Rotarians of Ohio. It was not compulsory that a Rotary Club should join this but later developments showed that they did so practically one hundred per cent.*

# The Need for a Decentralized System

Two years after figuring out how to approach the issue of helping disabled children, Allen had succeeded in forming, with the cooperation and interest of Ohio Rotary clubs, the Ohio Society for Crippled Children. The society, and Allen's work, had just begun.

Daddy Allen's memoirs:

*The next important move for Ohio was the question of a plan that . . . would carry out . . . the thought on which I was attempting to build a State movement, namely, the carrying of the facilities to the child, against the question of a State institution which had been started through Governor Cox.*

*I had gotten the idea from the experience that I had gone through at Gates Hospital that instead of bringing the children a long ways to the hospital, you had to bring the facilities to the child and not the child to the facilities. . . .*

*. . . a centralized institution, whether it be in Columbus or in Elyria would take only so many, but if we could establish in, not one center, but in ten, scattered throughout different sections of the state, and have those institutions properly safeguarded as to personnel, why we would be carrying out as far as we could with safety, the thought of bringing the facilities to the child.*

*In that thought the problem of the crippled child goes back to every town in the State, and it is the interest that is aroused and kept alive there that has so much to do with the future of the crippled child in that community.*

# Some Historical Perspective

The prevailing opinion at that time was that people with disabilities should be cared for within institutions, if they were cared for at all. The first institution for people with disabilities, the Hospital for the Ruptured and Crippled, was opened by a group of surgeons in New York City in 1863. Just three years later, in 1866, a second hospital opened in that city, the New York Orthopedic Hospital and Dispensary, that also offered outpatient care for people with disabilities.

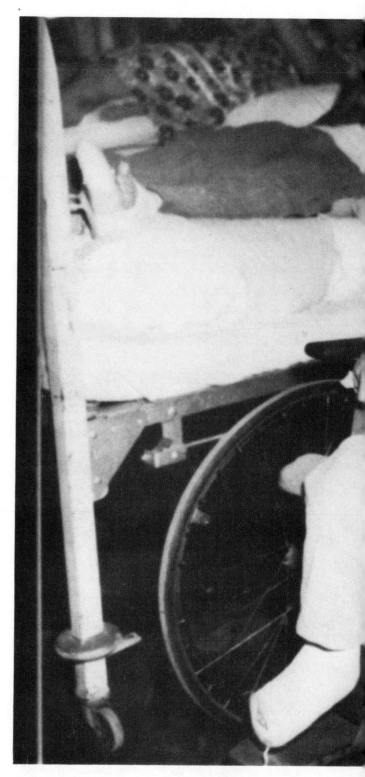

*Opening Christmas presents at Gates Hospital given by Rotary and other groups.*

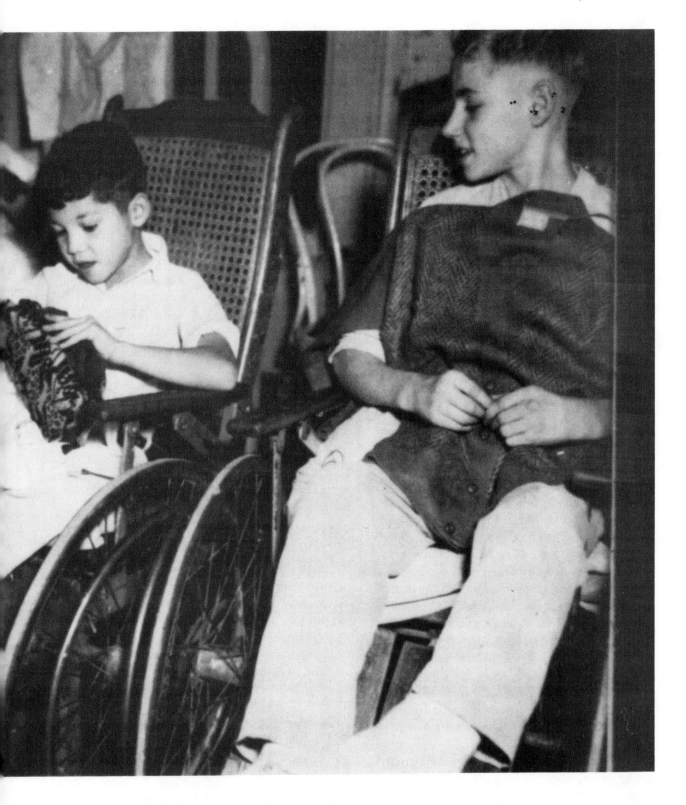

Throughout the country, primarily in urban areas, a sprinkling of similar hospitals for people with disabilities appeared. Some were public, some private. The care available included surgery, but the concept of rehabilitation hadn't yet developed to any great extent.

A few special "homes" that combined medical care and schooling were opened specifically for children with disabilities. The first was the Home of the Merciful Saviour in Philadelphia in 1884.

There were also a few private, nonresidential schools created for children with disabilities—specifically, the Industrial School for Crippled and Deformed Children, established in Boston in 1893, and special day schools established in 1898 in New York by the Children's Aid Society.

The Minnesota state legislature established the first state-run hospital and home for children with disabilities in 1879. New York followed suit in 1900 and Massachusetts in 1906 with a state-run hospital school.

In addition, the first public school classes for children with disabilities opened in 1900 in both Chicago and New York.

Before 1914 four states owned and maintained institutions for people with disabilities—New York, Minnesota, Nebraska and Massachusetts. People generally assumed other states would follow suit in establishing state facilities for residents with disabilities. Ohio and Illinois had in fact passed legislative acts providing for such facilities, but, according to Harry Howett, writing in *Better Health* magazine in 1926, "after careful investigations of the problem of the cripple, decided not to build them."

So some care was available to people with disabilities, and even specifically to children having disabilities, but it was by no means comprehensive or widespread. The care that did exist at the time, however, was actually evidence of quite progressive, very modern social thinking.

The early settlers in this country had maintained, for approximately two hundred years,

the customs and practices they had brought with them from Europe, and mostly from England. Those practices included putting children or adults with disabilities into almshouses along with paupers and the mentally and physically ill. People generally expressed repugnance toward those who had deformed or misshapen bodies, and therefore hid them away, shunned them and gave them alms.

These attitudes began to change somewhat during the second half of the 1800s. This was due in part to advances in medical science and the development of surgery, and partly due to a growing humanitarian interest and more sophisticated understanding that people with disabilities still had normal feelings and normal intelligence.

This was the world, then, into which Daddy Allen was introducing the Ohio Society for Crippled Children, with its concept of decentralized care for all children with disabilities, wherever they could be found. Allen's vision was truly new and truly revolutionary.

# Need for Legislation

Daddy Allen knew that his Ohio society wouldn't be able to accomplish its goals without funding from the state, so in his characteristic way he immediately appointed a committee to work on suitable legislation. Here's how he explained the process:

*The thought that had come to my mind and . . . was quite revolutionary was to get . . . that class of legislation whereby . . . the handling of the program and work for crippled children would be through the Department of Welfare and . . . the actual financing responsibility for the child would be thrown back to the different counties of the State. . . .*

*We concerned ourselves first with the right piece of machinery. . . . My thought was that . . . we could work out some legislative program whereby the State of Ohio would furnish the price of care, treatment and education, and private philanthropy would furnish the facilities. . . .*

*[Allen's associates drafted a bill in which] . . . the state of Ohio, through our Welfare Department, would set up a rotating fund . . . and . . . this law should allow the different counties of the state to appropriate in their budgets a certain amount in behalf of the treatment of crippled children.*

*The idea . . . was put in proper form and . . . presented . . . as House Bill 157 . . . . There was another piece of legislation . . . whereby the different municipalities under proper supervision from the Department of Education would establish . . . special schools or classes for crippled children. . . .*

As commonly happens with proposed legislation, these bills stalled in committee. But the Ohio legislature didn't know what it was dealing with when it stalled something of Daddy Allen's! Allen was above all things a man of action, and he quickly taught other members of Rotary and the Ohio society how to be men of action themselves, as well as tough lobbyists—as the following account demonstrates:

*These two pieces of legislation went before the House and Senate [in the spring of 1920]. They were passed on the first reading, and then there was a lull . . . and our legislation was in the hands of a committee and had never been reported out. I used to call it . . . a "pickling committee" who decided to put it in brine and not into effect.*

*[Allen later received a telegram from Harry H. Howett, from the Department of Welfare, stating that the legislation would likely never reach the floor before the House and Senate adjourned.]*

*Ohio governor signing legislation to assist people with disabilities.*

"That was rather a stunning blow, so I immediately called by phone the president of the Cleveland Rotary Club and asked him if he would get together his directors at noon that day and told him we must act quickly or we would be held up for perhaps two years. . . . The directors voted $1,000 from the funds of the Cleveland Rotary Club to be used immediately in telegraphing to the different Rotary Clubs of the state, 65 at the time, asking them, and their friends and their friends' friends to wire at once their representatives and Senator, urging the necessity of this legislation. . . .

The next day, Tuesday, there commenced to come in telegrams pretty lively; by Wednesday they were coming by the bushel basket load, and Thursday at eleven o'clock at night the two pieces of legislation that we had introduced were taken out of committee, "out of the brine," and passed by both the Senate and the House, as I remember, with no dissenting votes.

They were written into the statute books of the state of Ohio, and they have proved to be an influence affecting the lives of perhaps fifteen or twenty thousand children in this state and have presented an example that has been gradually followed by many states, provinces and nations in connection with the solution of the problem of the cripple.

# The Ohio Plan

Daddy and his associates got the necessary bills passed. This meant that the Ohio Plan, with its decentralized system of care for children with disabilities, went into effect. It was partially funded by the state of Ohio and partially by charitable contributions, mostly from Rotary.

Rotarians also saw to the actual functioning of the system—seeking out children with disabilities, and persuading their families to let them get medical attention.

The Ohio Plan was put into effect on Aug. 21, 1920. . . . We immediately went to work to develop different centers and were originally able to establish centers at Cincinnati, Dayton, Columbus, Akron, Youngstown, Toledo, Cleveland, and Elyria.

Later centers were established at Lima and Zanes-ville, the plan working through already existing, set-up hospitals, and with the proper personnel accepted by the Department of Welfare.

We cannot pay too much tribute to the Departments of Welfare, Health and Education of Ohio in their splendid cooperation and their arrangements to make the Ohio Plan really effective. . . .

. . . The interest of the different Rotary clubs throughout the state awakened people of many cities to the opportunity as well as the possibilities of service.

# The Human Touch

After Allen realized that the human touch was necessary to make this movement work, he quickly became a master at applying it. This excerpt about Allen's work in an issue of *The Rotarian*, dated October 1922, by Albert Sidney Gregg, describes his method for getting Rotary groups interested in his cause:

In selling the idea Allen would ask the club to pick out a crippled child and send it to the Gates Hospital for free treatment. That proposition always caught attention and won cooperation.

In Cleveland, Ruth Friedman, a girl of eight, was introduced to the Rotary Club. She was obliged to walk with her head down, with her hands touching her shoes. But in spite of her affliction she could bend her head around and look up and smile.

The girl was treated at Gates Hospital and as the result of two simple operations she was able to stand upright and get about with crutches. On the day she came back she walked down the aisle with crutches, head up and beaming with big smiles. She was lifted up onto the guest table where all could see her.

As the Rotarians realized what had been done to the girl, they forgot their meals and burst into unrestrained applause. It was a time of tears, handclapping and joy. That was a red-letter day for the Rotary people and for crippled children.

Effective as this technique was, there was nothing manipulative about it. Daddy Allen just knew that you couldn't simply talk about a worthwhile plan—you had to demonstrate its effectiveness in the lives of human beings.

So he visited Rotary after Rotary, and before long Ohio was abuzz with this new movement. The state government also showed a growing interest in the care of disabled children and began conducting surveys of their numbers and locations.

# The Gates Hospital

Gates Hospital—Daddy's memoirs:

*During this time [the early 1920s] there were many county surveys and many clinics for examination, arranged by the Department of Health and Welfare, and the mobilization of those forces revealed in many counties a condition which no one had understood.*

*The effect on Gates Hospital was the immediate filling of the institution. In fact we had children from many counties that later reported to the nearest center in which they lived. . . .*

*Gates Hospital was the first crippled children's hospital dedicated exclusively to crippled children between New York and Chicago, and was the first hospital . . . made possible by lay interest.*

# Firsthand Accounts of Gates

Although the following treatments may seem like ancient history when viewed in the context of the care available today for people with disabilities, they were used within the lifetime of many people still living. The accounts of three people who had firsthand experience with Gates Hospital—a woman who had been there as a young child and her

mother, and another woman who had been a patient at Gates twice, once for polio when she was a toddler, and later as a teenager with a dislocated hip—follow.

Joan Moore was a patient at Gates Hospital in 1936:

*When I was about two and a half I had surgery at Gates Hospital for a severe case of knock knees that was probably the result of rickets. I was in a full body cast and stayed there for almost eight months after my operation.*

*I was really young so I don't remember too much about it, but I do recall being wheeled outside in my bed to get fresh air—they believed that was very beneficial for us. I also remember I didn't like being in that body cast at all because I could barely move.*

*I think I must have been kind of a brat because I also know I wouldn't eat any jello or peas there even though I liked those foods.*

*One of the older patients, Netty, became my special friend and she was the only one I would let feed me. She was also the only one I'd quiet down for when I was crying.*

*I was born and raised in Elyria and my grandmother, who also lived in Elyria, remembered the big street car accident there in 1907—the accident that caused the death of Edgar Allen's son, Homer. She told me about that accident all the time and then she would say, 'You know that's the same man who formed the organization that helped you to walk.'*

*For the past two years I've been working for the Elyria Easter Seal Society as manager of the equipment and loan program and part-time in their respite program.*

*I never dreamed I'd be working for the same place that helped me walk when I was a kid.*

Dorothy Burns, Joan Moore's mother:

*It was during the Depression, in the late '30s, when my daughter Joan had this problem with her legs—probably rickets—and I myself was not doing too well either—times were hard.*

*I'm not quite sure exactly how they found out about Joan's condition but there was a lovely health service in Elyria and I think they were making a survey of children in the area. Joan was attending a little day nursery school at the time, kind of like a day care*

31

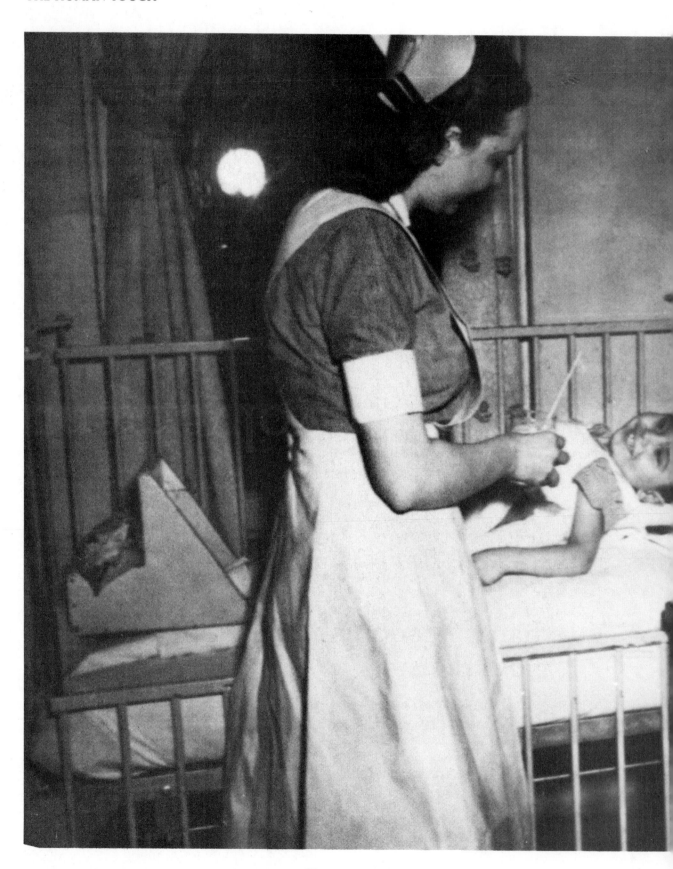

center, and I think they noticed the problem with her legs there.

She was admitted to Elyria Memorial Hospital for surgery on her legs, and then sent to Gates Children's Hospital (on the same grounds) to recuperate. They had to break both her legs for the surgery and just thinking about that still sends shudders through my body.

I remember when I came to the hospital the morning of the surgery a young girl, about 14 or so, asked me if I was Joan's mother. She told me not to tell anyone so she wouldn't get into trouble but Joan had been crying during the night and she felt so sorry for her she had gotten up and taken her into bed with her, where she then slept quietly the rest of the night. The girl was apparently also waiting for surgery there and didn't want to get in any trouble with the nurses for what she had done.

She was so sweet but I must say I never saw her again.

I visited Joan at Gates as much as I could and the children really seemed to like it there. It was a beautiful building with red brick and white columns and a solarium. It's a shame it was torn down—it was such a pretty place.

The nurses were quite nice and I think they thoroughly spoiled the children there. I don't think any child ever complained about being at Gates Hospital.

I had some neighbors who kind of criticized me for sending Joan to Gates for treatment. Their daughter had a problem with one of her hands but they would often point out how they were taking care of their daughter on their own, kind of taking a jab at me for not handling Joan myself.

Well, Joan now has straight legs and no remnant of her earlier problem while those neighbors' daughter still has a hand she can't move.

I had decided back then and I still believe now that sometimes you have to do painful things in order to gain something else. The birth of anything is painful and carrying out any idea is painful. Wearing that body cast was painful for Joan but she can verify that it was worth it and that the Easter Seal program is just wonderful.

Nurse and patient at Gates Hospital.

Netty Clark was a patient at Gates Hospital in 1936:

*When I was a child I stayed at Gates Hospital twice. The first time was when I was two or three and had polio, and then again, in about 1936, when I was 16 and had surgery for a dislocated hip.*

*I don't remember much about my first time there, but I remember enjoying myself a lot when I went back there as a young girl.*

*For one thing there hadn't been too many girls in the neighborhood where I lived but at the hospital there were quite a few girls for me to be friends with and we had a great time together.*

*We usually had between four and six girls in a ward, and after visiting hours were over, we would put on these performances.*

*We'd turn out all the lights except one at somebody's bed. That girl would move the light around so it was like a spotlight on her. She would put on a little act, and then it would be the next girl's turn.*

*Girls who could walk but maybe had some problems with their arms would do a little dance. And kids like me, who couldn't walk, would sing or tell a story or maybe talk about something that had happened to us sometime.*

*Sometimes we just turned out all the lights and told ghost stories and got ourselves all scared. We had a lot of fun.*

*Those of us who wanted to read after lights out would put a flashlight under the covers and read like that. Once one of the girls scorched her sheet doing that. We could all smell the fabric starting to burn, so we got up and changed the sheets before any of the nurses found out. And as far as we could tell, they never did find out or at least never said anything about it.*

*I also remember being Joan Moore's special friend. She was so little when she was there and she cried a lot at night so I would hold her hand until she went to sleep. This went on for a couple of months, until one night the head nurse was on night duty and when she found out what I was doing she told me that had to stop. Joan cried a lot that first night, but then she got used to falling asleep by herself. We stayed friends, though, and I visited her a lot.*

Former Gates Hospital patient Joan Moore standing in front on left after legs were straightened. (Courtesy Joan Moore)

*Tutors came and taught us our lessons and we also had arts and crafts classes. I still have a tablecloth I made there, except it's kind of stained, and a stuffed cat which is now very dilapidated.*

*When I was there I was young and in a playful mood most of the time, so I didn't really think much about where the source of all this help was coming from. But when I got older I realized it was Easter Seals that had helped me so much and I went and taught arts and crafts classes at the local society for a couple of years.*

*Actually Easter Seals is still helping me. I use a walker sometimes now and a wheelchair the rest of the time. With my current financial situation I couldn't afford to buy the chair I needed. Easter Seals told me the right sources to contact in order to get it. Easter Seals has helped me in a lot of ways.*

# The Movement Grows

Even without today's media techniques and the heightened speed by which information travels, the work of the Ohio society became known rather quickly across the country.

As Allen explained:

*The immediate effect and the number of children that were being handled in Ohio through this plan . . . attracted the attention of other States, and so in the fall of 1921 the Ohio Society took the leadership in a movement to bring together interested people from Michigan, New York, Illinois, and Ohio, and called a meeting at Toledo for the . . . purpose of discussing . . . whether this movement should develop outside of Ohio in the form of a larger organization. . . .*

*All were pretty impressed and interested and there seemed to be a pretty unanimous sentiment to take the Ohio Plan as guide for other states . . .*

*And then there was organized the National Society for Crippled Children which elected officers of which the first president was Edgar F. Allen, the Vice President Hugh Van de Walker, and a board of directors made up of Michigan, New York and Illinois people.*

*At that time the next question was how to put into action what we had decided to do.*

Daddy Allen made a smooth transition from local community involvement to state-wide responsibility and rather quickly national leadership, with little or no comment. For him, apparently, as the job grew larger, so too did his vision and his willingness to take on greater and greater responsibility.

To develop the organization on a national scale, Allen did essentially the same thing he did when developing the society in Ohio. He worked long hours, he traveled constantly, he went to meeting after meeting of Rotary in other states and he talked unceasingly to people about the movement and how they could become part of it. He dedicated all his waking hours, and the rest of his life, to it.

A 1924 issue of *The Crippled Child*, the magazine published by the national society, offered the following description covering only a three-month period from Daddy Allen's journal.

*Traveled 6,900 miles ... On sleeper 25 nights ... away from home 44 days ... Spoke at 27 Rotary meetings ... Attended 5 annual meeting of State Societies ... Met men from 100 Clubs ... Held many extra meetings of committees ... Letters answered run to thousands ... Am building up statistics ... Organized Virginia ... Prepared many papers for State Departments ... Visited 21 Reconstruction Homes and Schools ... When not busy raise money to help H. E. Van de Walker, treasurer; never less than $100 a month, some months $1,000 ... No time off—8 to 16 hours a day ... Feeling fine—62 years old May 8th ... Keep on Keeping On.*

Word continued to spread, state after state joined the national society and by the following year, the organization had become the International Society for Crippled Children, with affiliates in Canada, and hopes of spreading the movement worldwide (although in 1939, for several reasons including the demands of management and coordination, the society returned to being only a national organization).

Thousands of children with disabilities were receiving treatment and assistance, largely because Daddy Allen had met Jimmie Bodak, and Daddy Allen was the way he was.

# III
# Funding the National Society: The Seals

*F*rom Daddy Allen's memoirs:

*The question of financing the State Society . . . has been and is still somewhat of a problem, and we have . . . tried this and that and the other with more or less success.*

*It has been very difficult to bring before the people the needs of a State Society financially, but when we stop to consider the value of such an organization and the results that could be obtained through such an organization there should be just the reverse.*

During the 1920s Daddy Allen's idea—the acorn—had grown into a slender young tree with healthy roots and branches—a network of affiliates across the continent and abroad, serving children with disabilities.

But the tree needed sustenance to grow and mature. Daddy Allen's organization, like all organizations, needed money to do its work.

State funds for people with disabilities were still scanty or nonexistent during those years. That meant that the society had to survive on its contributions, which came mostly from Ohio Rotary clubs and individual memberships of varying amounts.

But those contributions weren't generating enough income to support the work that needed to be done.

In its first ten years, from 1921 to 1931, the society had raised, and spent, only $200,000, an average of $20,000 a year—scarcely enough to meet its goal of helping children with disabilities all over the world!

And in the early '30s, with the nation sliding more deeply into the Depression, even those contributions began to decline sharply. Clearly, something needed to be done, and quickly. But what?

Paul H. King, then chairman of the society's finance committee (and successor to Daddy Allen as society president) suggested an annual sale of seals—small decorative stamps, like miniature posters—to help support the society.

Some board members were skeptical, but the national society and several affiliates decided to give this concept a try and launched the first Easter Seal campaign in the spring of 1934.

Selling seals was not a totally new approach to fundraising. The National Tuberculosis Association had successfully raised money for several years by asking for contributions for its Christmas seals. And since Easter was a time for new growth and renewed life, King felt the Easter season would be the best time to sell seals to help children with disabilities.

"Thoughts of Easter and the crippled child harmonize wonderfully," King said, ". . . and certainly the rehabilitation of crippled children means new life and activity."

A cartoonist at the *Cleveland Plain Dealer*, J. H. Donahey, designed the first seal, which showed a child on crutches in front of a large white cross.

In describing his design, Donahey said, "Simplicity seems most appropriate, since the crippled child asks simply for the right to live a normal life. Enduring physical handicaps, the causes of which science may someday conquer and control, this child commands the center of a white cross, expressing civilization's devotion to a program of rebuilding human frames and dedicating its efforts to

*Children helping to mail out Easter Seals at Gates Hospital.*

prevention."

The public responded to the seals enthusiastically. Even President Franklin Roosevelt sent a note to King that stated, "I write now to commend the movement . . . to arouse national consciousness in behalf of the crippled child and to raise funds for his care and general welfare. Good luck and success to you."

Just eight states—affiliates in Michigan, Ohio, Kentucky, Illinois, California, Texas, Pennsylvania, Arkansas—and Washington, D.C., participated in the first sale of Easter Seals, which raised about $47,000. More than half of that amount ($28,000) came out of Kentucky.

A. H. Thompson, a board member of the Kentucky society who organized that state's Easter Seal campaign, worked to make the seals available to as many people as possible. He understood that people were generally eager to contribute to this cause, and the buying of seals enabled them to participate in as modest or as generous a fashion as they could.

"The penny seal is the finest method in the world of telling your story and winning friends in a cause like ours, because it gives everyone a chance, from the newsboy to the millionaire horseman, to make his contribution. And once having given he will never forget he is helping crippled children," Thompson said.

The success of the seal campaign, that first year and in the years following, indicated that Thompson was right. The sale of seals through direct mail has continued to be a major fund-raising source for the society.

In addition to raising funds, the seals have

also raised awareness of the issues facing people with disabilities, as well as the kinds of help available to them. In the years following the first sale of seals, and continuing since then, increasing numbers of people have sought help for their disabilities through Easter Seals and received it!

From the very beginning, the seals spurred unprecedented expansion of the society as well as the growth of a nationwide movement on behalf of people with disabilities.

By 1940, hospital admissions of people with disabilities had almost doubled from 1934, enrollment in special classes had more than doubled as did the number of teachers in special schools. The entire field of rehabilitation began to gain acceptance and stature, and the numbers of orthopedic surgeons, physical and occupational therapists and other rehab professionals correspondingly began to increase dramatically.

The seals have no monetary value. They are, after all, just little pieces of sticky paper with pretty designs and pictures. But what they represent, and what they have helped to bring about, is vast and rich indeed. They have become universally recognized as tokens of a community service program the public is willing to support. They represent a commitment to improve the quality of life for people with disabilities. They have even given the National Easter Seal Society its name. And, most important, they have given all who wish it the opportunity to have a part in the ongoing process of empowering people who have disabilities.

# Designers of Easter Seals

| | | | | |
|---|---|---|---|---|
| 1934 | J. H. Donahey, Cleveland | | 1957 | Earl Gross, Chicago |
| 1935 | J. H. Donahey, Cleveland | | 1958 | Earl Gross, Chicago |
| 1936 | J. H. Donahey, Cleveland | | 1959 | Gerald Carveth & William Eads, Chicago |
| 1937 | Donald Croly, Detroit | | 1960 | Mrs. Ginny Winter, Chicago |
| 1938 | Hugh McNeill, Detroit | | 1961 | Daniel W. Keefe & James D. Webster, New York |
| 1939 | Robert Mallory, Elyria, Ohio | | 1962 | Robert Amft, Chicago |
| 1940 | E. B. Casebere, Dayton, Ohio | | 1963 | Don Marrs, Chicago |
| 1941 | T. Arthur Turner, Elyria, Ohio | | 1964 | Frank Boehm & Shannon Wheeler, Chicago |
| 1942 | T. Arthur Turner, Elyria, Ohio | | 1965 | Ted Giavis, New York, New York |
| 1943 | T. Arthur Turner, Elyria, Ohio | | 1966 | Mrs. Ruth Pratt Harasta, Johnson City, New York |
| 1944 | Raymond O. Whipple, Cleveland | | 1967 | Don Marrs, Leo Burnett Advertising, |
| 1945 | Barbara Bageman, South Pasadena, California | | 1968 | George Suyeoka, Leo Burnett Advertising, Chicago |
| 1946 | Mary Snyder, Memphis, Tennessee | | 1969 | George Suyeoka, Leo Burnett Advertising, Chicago |
| 1947 | Frank Gross, Janesville, Wisconsin | | 1970 | George Suyeoka, Leo Burnett Advertising, Chicago |
| 1948 | G. Don Ball, Chicago | | 1971 | Townsend Artman, Leo Burnett Advertising, Chicago |
| 1949 | Barney Lattin, San Leandro, California | | 1972 | Mike Vanezia, Leo Burnett Advertising, Chicago |
| 1950 | Ardy Kazarosian, Detroit | | 1973 | Don Marrs, Leo Burnett Advertising, Chicago |
| 1951 | National Easter Seal staff | | 1974 | Don Marrs and Ink Studio, Chicago |
| 1952 | National Easter Seal staff | | | |
| 1953 | Otis Shepard & Hubert Nelson, Chicago | | | |
| 1954 | Earl Gross & Edward T. Ryerson, Chicago | | | |
| 1955 | Earl Gross & Edward T. Ryerson, Chicago | | | |
| 1956 | Otis Shepard & Hubert Nelson, Chicago | | | |

1975 Don Marrs and Mike Vanezia, Chicago

1976 Gene Mandarino, Leo Burnett Advertising, Chicago

1977 Mike Vanezia, Leo Burnett Advertising, Chicago

1978 Mike Vanezia, Leo Burnett Advertising, Chicago

1979 Mike Vanezia, Leo Burnett Advertising, Chicago

1980 Permission Canadian Council for Crippled Children (Easter Seal Society)

1981 Mike Vanezia, Leo Burnett Advertising, Chicago (Permission Canadian Council)

1982 National Easter Seal Society staff—(featured was the 1982 National Easter Seal Child, Mary Sacco)

1983 National Easter Seal Society staff designed Seal—(featured was the 1983 National Child, Matt Huston)

1984 National Easter Seal Society staff—(featured was the 1984 National Child, Stephanie Swiney—this was also the 50th anniversary of the seal)

1985 National Easter Seal Society staff—(featured was the 1985 National Child, Danielle Newman Sibley)

1986 National Easter Seal Society staff—(featured was Jamie Brazzell, the 1986 National Child)

1987 Grant Jacoby, Inc., Chicago, offered a stylized lily and 1987 National Easter Seal Child, Susie Wilcox

1988 Campbell-Mithun-Esty Advertising, Minneapolis. Two seal designs were offered: a stylized lily and the 1988 National Easter Seal Child, Shawn Dennsteadt

1989 Campbell-Mithun-Esty Advertising, Minneapolis, designed the seal using the 1989 National Easter Seal Child, Joy Hall, and other seals offered were six artists' renditions of the lily. The artists were Heather Cooper, David Csicsko, Jozef Sumichrast, Jack Malloy, Gary Kelley and Dugald Stermer.

1990 Campbell-Mithun-Esty Advertising, Minneapolis. Features the 1990 Easter Seal Child, Vanessa Vance and the 1990 Adult representative, Key Stewart. The other seal offers six artists' versions of the lily. The artists were Michael Schwab, Mary O'Keefe Young, Cindy Berglund, Mark Fox, Gretchen Shields and Jim Dryden.

# Sometimes the worst thing about having a disability is that people meet it before they meet you.

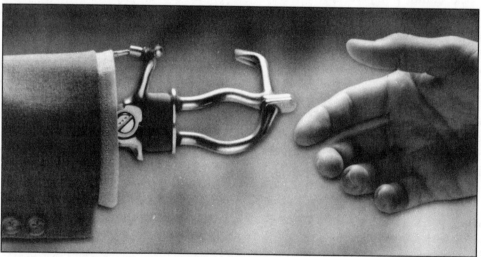

Remember, a person with a disability is a person first.
Awareness is the first step towards change.

# IV
# Easter Seal Programs

*T*he work of Easter Seals is divided into three main categories—direct services, public education and advocacy and research. Daddy Allen spoke of the importance of each of these, although he certainly could not have imagined the range and scope of each area today.

## Direct Services

From Daddy Allen's memoirs:

*There must be aroused within the State everywhere that local interest in the crippled child . . . [to] develop a program . . . not only [for] physical care but vocational training and education and follow-up service that was necessary to get the maximum results.*

Direct services describes Easter Seal activities that personally involve people with disabilities—different therapies to help with

*"Sometimes the worst thing about having a disability is that people meet it before they meet you."*

movement or speech, counseling, camping and recreation programs, equipment loan, computer-assistive technologies and other forms of technological assistance, job evaluation and training, infant stimulation programs, even day care for children with disabilities and their non-disabled peers. Direct services make up the heart—the human touch—of Easter Seals.

Currently, about 60 percent of the people who receive direct services from Easter Seals are under 21, with 40 percent over that age. The services available depend upon the needs of each community.

People of all ages and with disabilities from any cause—disability at birth, disease, accidents, or the aging process—can come to Easter Seals for the assistance they need. Easter Seals does not refuse service because of financial limitations.

Direct services can also be Model Programs. These are state-of-the-art programs offered at selected locations that try out new approaches to dealing with various disabilities, often incorporating new technology and the latest findings from recent research.

Model Programs currently include a Work Recovery program in Sarasota, Florida, aimed toward a quick return to work after injury or illness or, when necessary, toward adapting to a new job. There are computer-assisted technology sites that provide individually tailored computer systems to help people with disabilities at school or work. The Farm Family Rehabilitation Management program addresses the need of injured agricultural workers to return to their family farms with the help of adaptive technologies. And a new Head Trauma model program constitutes a new approach to long-term rehabilitation services for people who have had brain injuries.

To some extent, the disabilities people have today reflect the more complicated, technological society we live in, and therefore the nature of many direct services has changed over the years. Easter Seal centers now work more frequently with children who have cerebral palsy, neurological disorders, or spina bifida, for example, than with children disabled by diseases such as polio or rickets, both of which used to be common. Today babies with disabilities come to Easter Seals, saved at birth by modern technology, who would have died in the early part of the century.

Modern medicine now also saves many people from a variety of accidents and injuries that decades ago would have been fatal. These people also receive rehabilitation services.

An increasing number of older adults are also benefiting from Easter Seal services. Because people are living longer now, many develop the kind of disabilities that often occur with aging: stroke, heart attack and difficulties with walking, hearing and seeing.

During my ten years as host of the Easter Seal Telethon, I've personally visited a number of these centers specializing in helping older adults and people who have had strokes. I don't mind admitting to some powerful emotions as I watched wonderfully accomplished and valuable people fighting back from monumental setbacks, with the patient and loving help of Easter Seal volunteers and staff.

Whatever the age, whatever the disability, Easter Seals is there with direct services.

Helping children and older people with disabilities in every possible way is the main objective of Easter Seals, but as Daddy Allen found when he built the first hospital in Elyria, education and advocacy are necessary as well, possibly even taking precedence over the providing of facilities and direct services. Unless people understand the reasons and methods of rehabilitation, and really perceive why public help is needed, the programs might go nowhere.

If you look up the word "advocate" in the dictionary, you'll find that the word refers to someone who "pleads the cause of another in a court of law" or who "defends, vindicates, or espouses a cause by argument; an upholder; a defender." From its earliest beginnings, and by its very nature, Easter Seals has been an advocate for people with disabilities.

And it will remain an advocate until all persons who leave its programs can then go on to find jobs, housing, accessible transportation and the kind of lives they have a right to.

Daddy Allen clearly understood that the efforts of his society would not succeed on good will and hard work alone. The work at hand required financial support from the state, and disabled people needed protection under the law. Both things are still true.

The first thing Allen did after forming the Ohio society was lobby the Ohio legislature for laws to help with the treatment and education of its residents with disabilities.

As state after state joined the national society, Allen and his Rotary associates worked with each new state legislature, examining existing laws that might already focus on people with disabilities, and drafting bills for additional laws when needed.

*"This family is only welcome in somebody else's neighborhood."*

# This family is only welcome in somebody else's neighborhood.

When it comes to having a group home in their neighborhood, many people are more concerned about property value than human value. It's time we made room for everybody. Awareness is the first step towards change.

Easter Seals ®

# What's more paralyzing is the way he gets treated.

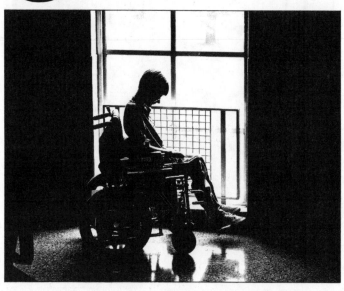

The hardest part about having a disability is being constantly reminded
that you have one. Sometimes that happens when people stare at you.
Or point at you. Or don't even think of including you in every day activities.
Maybe it's time to start treating people with disabilities like people.

Easter
Seals
®

A believer in the human touch, as we've already seen, Allen often met with the governors and legislators of the states that joined the national society.

The description of Allen's encounter with Governor Alfred Smith in New York is particularly enjoyable:

*I remember going to see Governor Alfred Smith who was governor at the time this legislation was being thrashed out in the legislative halls. . . . I had an appointment with him which did not last but a very few minutes and I remember his saying to me when I went into his office, "Yes, I know who you are. You are this fellow from out in Ohio and if those legislative enactments ever get to my desk, I am going to sign them. Goodbye."*

*I said, "Just a minute please. When you do sign them, will you use two pens and send me one of them?"*

*That was the extent of the conversation but in two weeks I got one of the pens.*

During the 1920s and into the '30s the legal foundation of the national society was built with the bricks of many state laws. At the same time the federal government was also beginning to show interest in the problems of people with disabilities, primarily in response to the many veterans who had returned home from World War I with a variety of disabilities.

Concern over the plight of the veterans generated the first federal law dealing with disabled people—the Vocational Rehabilitation Act of 1920. It provided work-related rehabilitation defined as "the rendering of a person disabled fit to engage in remunerative occupation," but was not highly funded.

The federal government again expressed concern with the well-being of the nation's citizens in 1930, when President Hoover convened a White House Conference on Child

*Advocacy poster: "What's more paralyzing is the way he gets treated."*

Health and Protection, involving 3,000 delegates from the fields of medicine, education and social work.

Conference members wrote and adopted a Bill of Rights for the Handicapped Child, which essentially stated that disabled children had a right to as full a life as possible, with access to medical treatment, rehabilitation and education in addition to "comradeship, love, work, play, laughter and tears."

The conference also suggested a comprehensive plan to help guarantee that children with disabilities would actually be given their rights. The plan outlined a system that called for the discovery and early diagnosis of disabilities, treatment, education, vocational training, protective legislation and research. It also recommended that the federal government give grants in aid to states that would carry out the plan.

As lawmakers began drafting the first Social Security legislation, members of the national and state societies lobbied hard for and succeeded in getting included in the Social Security Act of 1935 the provisions of the plan outlined for disabled children at the White House conference.

Title V, Part 2 of the Social Security Act describes the services available to disabled children and the grants allotted to states to provide those services.

Since the '30s, Easter Seal representatives have continued to work closely with federal lawmakers both for the passage of laws that help guarantee the rights of disabled people, and in opposition to proposed laws that would infringe on these rights or the ongoing work of Easter Seals and kindred organizations.

In 1973 Easter Seals opened an Office of Governmental Affairs in Washington, D.C. The staff monitors legislation and works for the passage of laws that would improve the quality of life for people with disabilities. The Washington office is concerned with legislation covering a variety of issues: health care, education, housing, transportation and technology.

Since it opened, this office has worked behind the scenes fostering the passage of the following laws:

- The Rehabilitation Act of 1973, which guarantees basic civil rights for people with disabilities in all federal and federally funded programs.
- PL 94-142, The Education for All Handicapped Children Act, which guarantees a free, public education for all children and mandates "mainstreaming" or the "least restrictive environment" for all children.
- The Rehabilitation, Comprehensive Services and Developmental Disabilities Amendment of 1978, which expands the federal government's responsibility for providing vocational rehabilitation services and for funding of independent living centers and special recreation projects.
- Fair Housing Amendment Act of 1986, which requires new buildings and remodeled older buildings, when possible, to meet minimum standards of accessibility for people who are disabled.
- Air Carrier Access Act of 1986, which makes it illegal to discriminate against passengers with disabilities.
- The Americans with Disabilities Act extends basic civil rights to all people with disabilities into the private sector.

Life for people with disabilities in the United States of America would be much different if the above legislation hadn't been enacted and facilitated. Easter Seals has made a tremendous difference.

Easter Seal advocacy extends beyond the courtroom, however, and into the homes of the general public through its many public education and advocacy programs. These programs highlight disability issues and people with disabilities in everyday activities.

They focus on what all people have in common. Recent public advocacy programs—conceived, funded and produced by corporate sponsors and Easter Seals' ad agency, Campbell-Mithun-Esty, Advertising, Minneapolis—include:

- *Friends Who Care*, an award-winning disability awareness campaign for nondisabled junior and senior high school students. The original campaign was funded by Enesco Corporation. A grant from Ronald McDonald Children's Charities made it possible to expand the Friends Who Care program and include 20,000 third- and fourth-grade classrooms identified by Easter Seal Societies and Centers for Independent Living nationwide.
- *A Safe Home is No Accident*, media scripts and a brochure checklist for safeguarding homes against hazards that can cause accidents and disabling injuries. Funded by Century 21 Real Estate Corporation.
- *Are You Listening to What Your Child May Not Be Saying*? a brochure, ads and media scripts serving as guides for parents to early indicators of potential developmental delays or disabilities in young children. Funded by Amway Corporation.
- *Awareness is the First Step Towards Change* is Easter Seals' newest multi-media advocacy campaign. Developed to reflect the enactment of the 1990 Americans with Disabilities Act, "The First Step" is designed to point out all the subtle and not-so-subtle ways in which people with disabilities are still discriminated against when they look for employment, or housing, or transportation. "The First Step" was created with Campbell-Mithun-Esty and made possible by Enesco Corporation.

*Advocacy poster: "Actually, names hurt as much as sticks and stones."*

# Actually, names hurt just as much as sticks and stones.

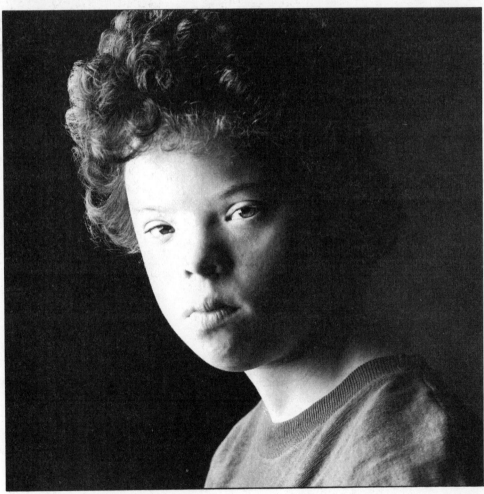

When you're mentally retarded, you get called all kinds of things.
And that's not the worst of it. Because after awhile, you can start believing that what people say is true. And that there really is something wrong with you.
Because no matter what anyone says, names really can hurt someone. Permanently.

# Nobody pushes Mike around.

He gets to school just fine. Plays games well. Has lots of friends.
With the help of Easter Seals, there's hardly anything he can't do on his own.
Except maybe his math homework. Support Easter Seals.

Easter
Seals ®

## Give The Power To Overcome.

# Attitudes

The fact is that certain attitudes, certain notions, can be just as handicapping to people with disabilities as architectural barriers. It may sound strange, but the barriers people create within their own minds about people with disabilities can block the way for them as much as, and sometimes even more than, the most formidable flight of stairs or the narrowest doorway.

These attitudinal barriers are not only as limiting as physical barriers, but they can sometimes be more difficult to change or remove.

The attitude that creates the biggest handicap, the greatest barrier, is the notion that people with disabilities are not like other people.

It is not uncommon for people to unconsciously treat those with visible and verbal disabilities as if they were almost children, no matter how old they are. People fail to understand that those with disabilities have the same needs, wishes and desires as everybody else. The attitude that disabled people are essentially different creates a handicap, a barrier, that stifles communication, mutual understanding and the basic flow of everyday life between people who have disabilities and those who don't.

The truth is that people everywhere are more the same than they are different, regardless of how they move about, speak, see or hear.

To state it plainly: People with disabilities are just like everybody else. They want what most people want—respect, friendship, work and love. They have a wide variety of interests and talents—just like everybody else. And they like to do what most people like to do—

go out to work, travel, go to restaurants, see movies and plays, socialize, develop hobbies, participate in sports, be part of a family, have a circle of friends.

Using a wheelchair or braces or a hearing aid doesn't alter these basic desires. The desires come from within, and under the skin people are the same. The difference between people who have disabilities and those who don't are surface variations, addressing only a small part of the countless things that make up a human being.

Think about the language we use so often, as we talk about people with disabilities. There's a big difference, for example, between referring to someone as a "victim" of cerebral palsy or spina bifida (or whatever) and simply saying the person "has" cerebral palsy or spina bifida.

"Victim" is a loaded word bearing negative connotations of helplessness and suffering, and is therefore inaccurate, since people with cerebral palsy are not necessarily helpless nor do they always suffer.

When we say someone simply "has" a certain disease or condition, on the other hand, we avoid those negative connotations because "has" is a neutral term that states something without judgment or pity.

Some other words we ought to avoid because they create attitudinal barriers and have negative connotations are "afflicted," "invalid," "unfortunate," "pitiful," "poor," "deaf and dumb" and "crippled."

The word "crippled" was in earlier parts of this book a number of times. Daddy Allen used it constantly and in fact it was part of the name of the first Easter Seal Societies— the Ohio Society for Crippled Children and the National Society for Crippled Children, which then became the National Society for Crippled Children and Adults.

But, as you may have noticed, Easter Seals doesn't use the term "crippled" anymore. The change came about not simply as a matter of fashion, like the length of skirts or the width of ties, but because people with disabilities

*1990 print ad for national campaign.*

began to speak up against words like "crippled," "victim," "handicapped," and "wheelchair bound." They began letting people know such words were both inaccurate and possibly offensive, suggesting limitations and attributes they didn't necessarily have.

People with disabilities began pointing out, for example, that most "handicaps" come from external situations, such as stairs and narrow doorways that limit or deny access. Whether a disabling condition is handicapping or not frequently depends upon the environment people with disabilities occupy.

The words we use have a big influence on our perceptions, probably more than we realize. That old children's saying—"Sticks and stones may break my bones but names will never hurt me"—really isn't accurate. Names do hurt, labels do hurt. Referring to people with disabilities by names and labels is denying them their rightful dignity.

But when we choose our words carefully, accurately and non-prejudicially, our perceptions will in turn be careful, accurate and non-prejudicial. Our attitudes will be balanced.

And even though Daddy Allen himself used words like "crippled" and "handicapped," his heart was in the right place. And he, more quickly than almost anybody, would have benefitted and adjusted to what he learned about attitudes from the people with disabilities themselves.

# Accessibility

It is not an uncommon nightmare to be trying to get some place but you just can't, no matter how hard you try. Have you ever dreamed you were locked in somewhere, and you couldn't get out—or you were locked out, and couldn't get in?

These are common daytime experiences for people with disabilities. To an able-bodied person, a flight of stairs indicates a way in or out of a building. But to someone with a physical disability, it may say KEEP OUT.

To an able-bodied person, a curb on a street corner is something you simply step off to cross the intersection. But to someone with a physical disability, it may say YOU CAN'T CROSS HERE.

To an able-bodied person, plushy, spongy carpeting may be something nice to sink one's feet into. But to someone with a physical disability, it says STAY AWAY.

To an able-bodied person, a doorknob is something you grasp and turn to get in or out of a room or building. But to someone with a physical disability, a doorknob may be the same as a lock.

If you're an able-bodied person, you may never have considered that many aspects of your physical environment—stairs, curbs, carpeting, doorknobs, the height of public telephones—create impossible barriers to people with disabilities.

They're not the kinds of things people think too much about if they can move freely. But people whose movements are restricted can never stop thinking about them, because they face hundreds of these barriers, these KEEP OUT signs, every day, as they simply try to get from one place to another.

The whole truth about accessibility is that these barriers don't have to exist. In fact, changing some of the designs in our physical environment is perhaps the easiest, most effective means of bringing ability into disability.

These changes in our physical environment enable people with disabilities to live independent lives. These changes mean that disabled people can work, shop, tend to business and contribute to the society they are a part of.

For over thirty years now Easter Seals has been at the forefront of efforts to make our

*Advocacy poster: "Are you listening to what your child may not be saying?"*

# are you listening to what your child may not be saying

Sometimes our young children don't do things when we think they should. Most of the time, there's really no cause for worry. They're developing at their own pace.

So, how do you know when to be concerned? And where can you go for advice? Easter Seals can help.

"Are You Listening . . ." is a simple checklist for parents. It gives you an idea of what to look for as your child develops, and when to call for professional help. It's important to know, because early intervention can make a difference in your child's future.

For a free brochure, send a self-addressed, stamped envelope to The National Easter Seal Society, 70 East Lake Street, Chicago, Illinois 60601. Or contact the Easter Seal Society in your community.

Easter Seals
®

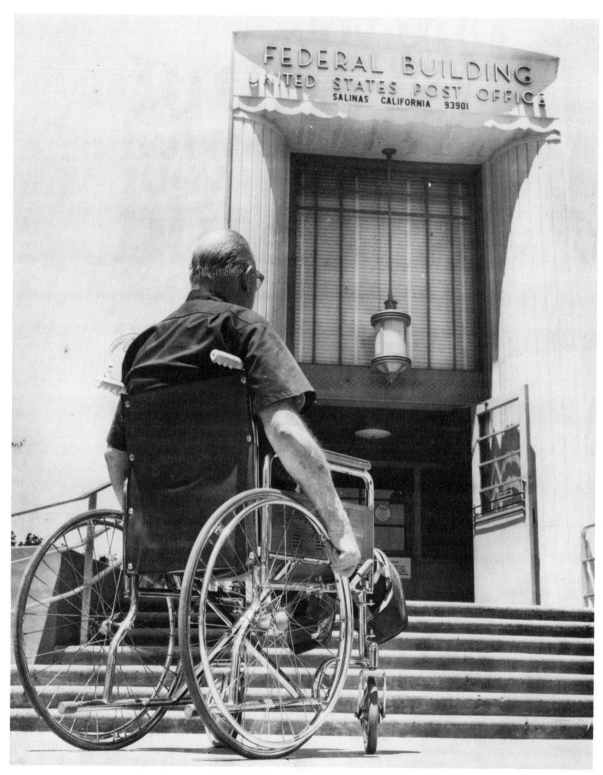

*Man in wheelchair facing steps outside a public building,
1977.*

physical environment accessible to people with disabilities.

Although wheelchairs have been around for over a hundred years, the concept of re-designing architectural barriers wasn't considered seriously until after World War II, when thousands of veterans were returning home with physical disabilities.

The movement stemmed in large part from the frustrations of people who worked in re-hab centers. Again and again they found that the disabled veterans they had rehabilitated couldn't get jobs simply because buildings were inaccessible.

By 1959, groups concerned about people with disabilities had sufficiently recognized the problem of environmental barriers, and they began taking action. Easter Seals, in fact, provided the main financial support for studies done in conjunction with the President's Committee on Employment of People with Disabilities to create and implement barrier-free architectural designs.

By 1961 these groups had co-authored "Making Buildings and Facilities Accessible to and Usable by the Physically Handicapped." The American National Standards Institute (ANSI) approved and adopted these new building specifications, entitled ANSI Standard A 117.1.

By 1967 federal legislation was recommended to implement the new ANSI standard in a report entitled "Design for All Americans," prepared by the National Commission on Architectural Barriers, published by the Department of Health, Education and Welfare. This led to the passage in 1968 of Public Law 90-480, which required publicly owned and federally financed buildings to be designed, constructed or altered to assure ready access and use by people with disabilities, according to specifications of the 1961 ANSI standards.

These specifications, with minor changes and additions, are still in use. They describe ways to construct both the interiors and exteriors of buildings so that people with disabili-

ties can enter a building, move about freely inside, use a bathroom, telephone, water fountain, elevator, open doors and get through doorways, conduct the business at hand and then exit freely, without assistance.

The changes required to make buildings and places accessible tend to be rather simple—ramps and elevators instead of stairs, cuts in the curbs, tightly woven carpeting or other kinds of flooring instead of plush carpeting, doorways and hallways wide enough to accommodate wheelchairs and levers instead of doorknobs.

But although the changes may be simple, most people recognize that eliminating architectural barriers has been one of main factors in providing the equality of rights constitutionally guaranteed to people with disabilities. These design changes actually facilitate movement for everyone, not only people with disabilities.

People tend to prefer walking up a ramp rather than stairs, if both are available. People pushing strollers and buggies, pulling wagons or delivery carts or riding bicycles certainly appreciate curb cuts. And people with their arms full of file folders, children, snacks or even grocery bags enjoy being able to push down a lever on a door, maybe with an elbow or an edge of a hand, rather than having to drop everything to twist a doorknob.

Children usually think the lower water fountains installed for people with disabilities were meant for them, not to mention the lower public phones for people with disabilities that also enable children to make their own calls—calls that sometimes can be very important.

The simple outline of a person sitting in a wheelchair is the international symbol of access. You see it in front of buildings, in parking lots and on bathroom doors. Rehabilitation International, comprising national and international organizations providing rehabilitation services for the disabled in more than 60 countries, adopted this symbol in 1969 at its 11th World Congress on Rehabilitation of the Disabled.

This figure is now used around the world as a symbol of accessibility, particularly to people in wheelchairs. It replaces the implied KEEP OUT signs that architectural barriers suggest.

# Research

*... [I]t is a wonderful thing ... to develop plans that will care for the cripples and it is a beautiful picture that we could paint of little crippled children going to the hospitals and later throwing away their braces and crutches and ... made well, but it will be a much more beautiful picture if through preventive measures we could tear down our hospitals and build school houses, raising children dedicated to the service of others and the elimination of disease throughout the land.*

Daddy Allen's first concern was setting up a community-based organization that would care for children with disabilities.

But that wasn't all he wanted. His dream included prevention and research. He believed, accurately, that medical research could find ways to eliminate some types of disabilities and, when eliminating them wasn't possible, could find better methods of treatment and rehabilitation.

The Easter Seal Research Foundation first began operating in the early 1950s, after the society had spent 30 years laying the groundwork for its programs and facilities throughout the country and was ready to pursue this new endeavor.

Since then, Easter Seals has helped fund hundreds of projects and scientific studies on a wide range of topics, including the effects of diseases, illnesses, accidents, rehabilitation, disability at birth and aging.

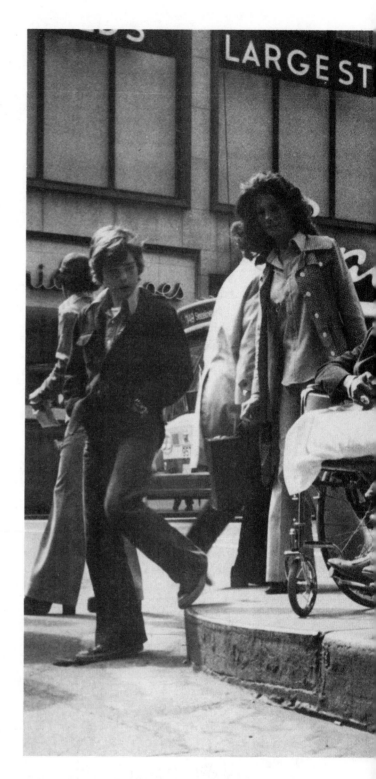

*People in wheelchairs demonstrate inaccessibility of State Street in downtown Chicago in 1976 as part of National Handicapped Awareness Week beginning May, 17, 1976. Left to right are William Passmore, board member of NESSCA; Lois Henneman, Committee for an Aware Chicago; Ralph "Jack" Powell, Paralyzed Veterans of America; and Frank DeGeorge, National Paraplegia Foundation.*

57

Some of the most recent studies have examined the effects of post-polio syndrome, measured the intellectual capacity of children with Down's syndrome, created resources for parents with disabilities and encouraged architects and engineers to create barrier-free environments.

Many of the projects have brought new insights into causes, treatment and possible prevention of different kinds of disabilities. Many have changed the lives of people with disabilities. And many are still under way, offering promises of greater understanding yet to be discovered. The Easter Seal commitment to finding new information to improve its services remains a vital part of the organization.

To those actively involved in Easter Seals' ongoing program, the first 71 years seem to have passed really quickly, and though direct services and advocacy have consumed most resources and energy, research is vital and will continue to play a large and growing role in the future of Easter Seals.

# V
# Easter Seal Volunteers

*T*he most moving part of the Easter Seal story is about the volunteers. When people, otherwise blessed and occupied with their own interests, reach out to help others, voluntarily and eagerly the real heartbeat in the human touch is felt.

Daddy Allen, in *The Rotarian*, 1922:

> *There is no other movement like this one . . . The personal service rendered by the Rotarians does the member almost as much good as it does the child. Many a Rotarian has found a new inspiration and a new kind of pleasure in helping some little fellow with a crooked arm or a bent leg to get a new grip on life.*

The joy of serving others lies at the heart of Easter Seals. The society began with volunteers, starting with Daddy Allen himself. It grew with their help, and it still depends on the many volunteers who donate their time, talent and energy so that people with disabilities can live more independent lives. Today there are thousands and thousands of people volunteering for Easter Seals in large and small ways, according to their abilities and availabilities.

For the last several years, in fact, over half a million people have volunteered some part of their time and resources to Easter Seals!

Without its volunteers, Easter Seals would not be here today. And without the countless hours amassed over 71 years of volunteer effort, it's hard to imagine how and whether a similar movement helping people with disabilities could have evolved.

Daddy Allen himself was a volunteer, as were the thousands of Rotarians and others who worked with him to organize the society across the country. For many Rotarians, volunteering meant the kind of dedication Allen described in a 1922 issue of the Rotary magazine:

> *On the date set for the examinations, members of the Rotary Club go to the homes of the crippled children and take them to the clinic. After the cases have been diagnosed and assigned to a hospital Rotarians are expected to follow the children right through and keep in close touch until the boys and girls have been cured or helped as far as possible, and taught something by which they may become self-supporting.*

As the years passed and the society grew, the volunteer corps expanded beyond mem-

*Black and white drawing of kids on a palm of a hand.*

bers of Rotary into thousands of people of all ages and from all walks of life who helped in a multitude of ways.

Volunteers now and in the past have been businessmen, housewives, factory workers, high school students, corporate executives, parents of children with disabilities, people with disabilities themselves, fraternities and sororities, service clubs, labor unions, professional organizations, tradespeople and celebrities.

They have held fund-raisers, sponsored scholarships, assisted with transportation of Easter Seal clients, served as aides to therapists and other professionals in Easter Seal centers, offered arts and crafts classes, underwritten projects and publications, worked on annual Easter Seal campaigns, served on government committees, helped establish Easter Seal policy, provided equipment and a host of in-kind services, taught daily living skills to people with disabilities, visited homes of Easter Seal clients, assisted with vocational training programs, helped stroke victims, worked to eradicate architectural barriers and, of course, served on Easter Seal boards of directors at the local, state and national levels.

In other words, volunteers just make the organization work!

The current chairman of the board of directors of the National Easter Seal Society, Walter A. Spencer, Jr., explained his volunteer involvement this way: "All of us who volunteer our time, energy and expertise to Easter Seals do so out of personal commitment. We all share the satisfaction of knowing that our efforts pay off. We can see how our Easter Seal programs allow people we know—adults and children with disabilities—to become as independent as they can be. We watch with pride as people move from our rehabilitation and therapy programs into the community—frequently on their own. With our camps and support groups, we know that Easter Seals is always there as a resource. We've come a long way in 71 years."

In my own ten-year involvement as telethon host I have seen wondrous changes, large and small, over and over again. I've stayed in touch, as best I can, with each of the National Children that have worked with me on the telethons, and have felt an almost parental rush of pride and tenderness as I've seen them grow and develop into responsible, capable young people. I've witnessed the progress of countless other kids I've met at the Easter Seal centers. I've watched the uphill but winning struggles of the adults who've had strokes or been injured. I've seen more and more people with disabilities on television and in movies and working at different jobs. And I've also seen a growing understanding of the needs and desires of people with disabilities and of how we can all work toward fulfilling those cherished goals.

I've seen that all those volunteer hours really do make a difference. And there really is no substitute.

The Bible says, and I believe the Bible, that what you give will be multiplied back to you. My efforts for Easter Seals have "paid off" for me many times over in terms of tremendous satisfaction and a deep joy. I think all other Easter Seal volunteers would agree that they have had similar rewards as a result of our work together.

And when I say "together," I mean that. This is really a team effort, and few of us could function productively in this massive effort without the contribution of each of the others.

The telethon wouldn't mean much, in spite of millions and millions of dollars raised, if we couldn't depend on countless man hours from hundreds of thousands of volunteers to work with the small paid and trained staff— to stretch those dollars to maximum productivity. And though the volunteers could accomplish a great deal without the proceeds of the telethon and other fund-raising efforts, they wouldn't have the buildings, the latest therapy equipment, the dedicated paid staff to guide their efforts. We are a team!

And finally, as I look back over a jam-packed, busy and fulfilling life (and I'm only getting started), I've come to a startling realization: there are only a few genuine highlights that stand out in the midst of all the other "busyness." To my amazement, those highlights aren't great career accomplishments—they're quieter moments of breakthrough in relationships, in life transformation, in spiritual growth. Everything else has already started to fade somewhat into the background.

And I'm sure that's true for all of us. Our life highlights, our most significant moments, are almost without exception those that affect the lives of others, that lift them higher somehow and help them see a new horizon.

So I, and most other Easter Seal volunteers, have signed on for the duration.

# VI
# Easter Seal Campaigns

*H*ow do you get a camel through the eye of a needle?

How do you condense a novel into ten choice words?

How do you make two hundred fifty million people aware of Easter Seals in ten seconds—or thirty minutes—or twenty hours?

Ours is an increasingly frantic, complex and distracted society. It's hard to get someone to focus on a message, no matter how important it is, because there are so many constant demands on our time and attention. Life is a constant hodgepodge of pressures, activities and distractions.

Because of this Easter Seals has contracted top advertising agencies including Leo Burnett (Chicago) and since 1988 Campbell-Mithun-Esty (Minneapolis) to help tell its story. Naturally, as society and mores and methods have changed year by year, so have the Easter Seal campaign messages. For that matter, even the way Easter Seals perceives its mission and how it presents its goals to a preoccupied people have changed.

Since the first sale of seals in 1934, Easter Seals has come to the public each year and

asked for its continued support in helping people with disabilities achieve maximum independence. In 1947 national and local child representatives became part of the campaign process, and in 1983 adult representatives also joined the yearly effort.

In the past, many of the fund-raising campaigns suggested that independence for people with disabilities meant throwing away their crutches. Some past campaigns referred to helping people walk, and some even mentioned miracles. There were a few campaigns that tugged unashamedly on heartstrings.

Easter Seals no longer describes its work in these ways nor does it view success in terms of total elimination of all disabilities. That would be an unrealistic, impossible goal and not quite the point of the Easter Seal organization.

The goal now and for the future is helping people with disabilities achieve maximum independence. Accordingly, a look at recent campaigns will show people with disabilities going about the regular activities of daily life.

In some recent Easter Seal posters a father holds his newborn infant, a best man stands

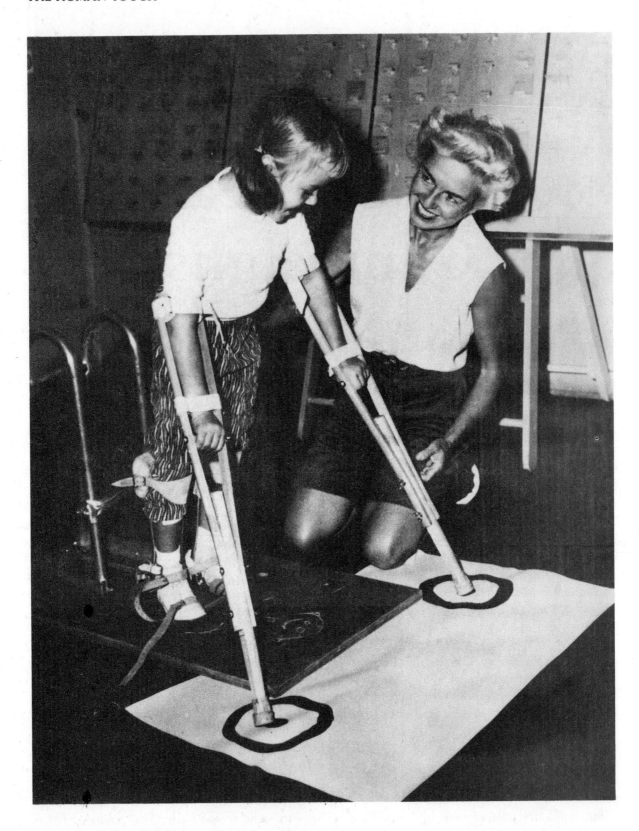

in a friend's wedding, a mother talks with her child.

The father has a prosthetic arm, but that's not the important part. What's important is that he's a dad, holding his child. The young man at the wedding stands with braces and crutches, but that's not really important. What's important is his being in the wedding party, serving as the best man. The mother and son are using sign language, but that's not the most important part. What's important is their communication, their talking together and bonding as mother and child.

The focus in these campaigns is on the people, not on the disability. The focus is on people involved in everyday activities. And Easter Seals is there to help make those activities possible for everyone.

The truth is that many people with disabilities will always need their crutches, but they can still be independent. Many will always need a wheelchair, but they can still be independent. And few, perhaps, may experience a miracle, but miracles aren't necessarily required for achieving independence. What is required is time, effort, hard work, research and funding.

Over the years Easter Seals has learned that people with disabilities can and do live independent, fulfilling lives using crutches, wheelchairs and other kinds of assistance. And Easter Seals is there to see that they reach maximum independence. Pity is neither sought nor welcome. Opportunity and independence are the objectives.

Jon Francks is paralyzed from the hips down as the result of a motorcycle accident. He lives a normal life and runs one of the fanciest and best health clubs in Los Angeles! He's its own best example of physical fitness!

Bob Wieland, a vet who lost his lower limbs in Vietnam, walked across the United States raising money for his favorite charities!

The Easter Seal campaign pictures are worth a thousand words. They show how Easter Seal campaigns have evolved over the decades. As the years progress, the campaigns begin more and more to portray people with disabilities within the context of everyday living—rather than isolated and on their own, perhaps looking up to the sky or standing in the palm of someone's hand, dependent or helpless.

The mission of Easter Seals has remained the same throughout its history, but its perception of success has matured.

*Girl learning proper placement of crutches, television photo ad, 1958.*

# The money you gave in 1971

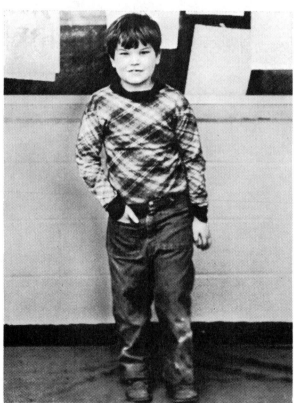

## walked in 1975!

**Help kids and adults, too!**

*Before and after photos used in 1975 Easter Seal
campaign.*

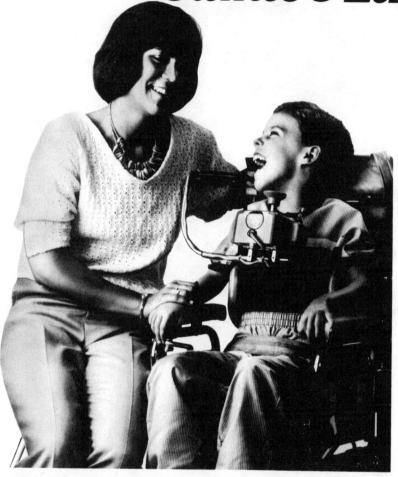

# "I Owe Easter Seals Jamie's Life."

"My son Jamie will never walk. But he's learned to deal with his disability with the help of the Easter Seal rehabilitation team. They gave him the emotional boost he needed to carry on his fight for independence. I do not believe Jamie would be the intelligent, optimistic and outgoing little boy he is today if so many people had not been involved in his critical early development.

*That's why I feel I owe Easter Seals Jamie's life.*"

*Denise Brazzell*

**Back a Fighter** **with Easter Seals**
*For people with disabilities*

*Photo of Jamie Brazzell and mother,*
*Denise, used in national ad campaign, 1986.*

**Stephanie is 8 years old.**
A spinal defect at birth left her paralyzed below the hips.

She walks with the aid of braces and crutches and has the fighting spirit to achieve a bright future.

Thousands of children like Stephanie...and adults, too... get the help they need from Easter Seals to carry on their fight for an independent life.

*Your help is needed, too.*

*National Child Stephanie Swiney in magazine photo ad, captioned, "She's Winning Her Fight for Independence."* in 1984 national ad campaign.

# PUT ABILITY IN DISABILITY

**The ability to learn, to teach, to earn, to mother, to create, to win, to laugh...**
Everyday in just about every community across America Easter Seals is helping someone with a disability take their first step, say their first word or share their first smile.

**Support**

*Easter Seals*®

These men, women, and children come to Easter Seals looking for a chance, not charity. Looking to put their lives and their dreams back together after a disabling accident or illness. Share in their work and aspirations. Help put ability in disability.

*Photo composite in 1987 print media national campaign.*

# After all we did for Pete, he walked out on us.

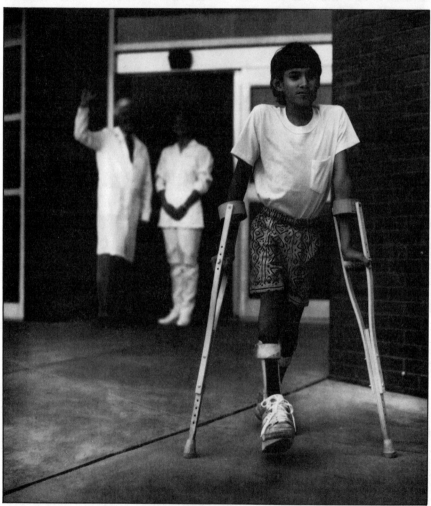

Learning to walk for Pete took a special kind of strength and determination. Plus the help of a lot of dedicated professionals. Nobody was happier when Pete walked out on them. Except maybe Pete. Support Easter Seals.

## Give The Power To Overcome.

Easter Seals ®

# VII
# National Easter Seal Children

*B*eginning in 1947, Easter Seals thought its campaign efforts would mean more if the public could get to know at least one specific child each year who had received Easter Seal services. This would help people realize their contributions were going to help individuals—with names and faces and personalities—rather than to some vast anonymous charity. This was another example of the human touch that Daddy Allen knew all about.

The boys and girls who became National Child representatives hailed from all parts of the country and had different kinds of disabilities. Each had a distinctive personality and charm. They were all a delight to work with. It's clear to me that my life would have been greatly enriched if I'd enlisted as a telethon host earlier.

One of the very best things about my involvement with Easter Seals has been getting to know and work with the National Child representatives and their parents. We share many memories of the funny things the kids said and did, of the nervous minutes waiting to meet the president and of the wonderful, glowing moments (and tiring hours) of the telethons.

These children, like all children, are growing up before my very eyes. And growing up in a way that makes me feel like a proud father. I see the older ones maturing and bit by bit taking on the new responsibilities of approaching adulthood. I see the younger ones doing well in school and enjoying sports and friends and all the other elements of childhood. I see each of their lives taking shape, and it makes me glad to have been a part of those lives.

*Print ad for 1990 campaign by Campbell-Mithun-Esty Advertising, Minneapolis.*

*1947 first National Child Harold Ferrell, age 15,
cerebral palsy.*

*1948 National Child Mike Golden, age 16, cerebral palsy.*

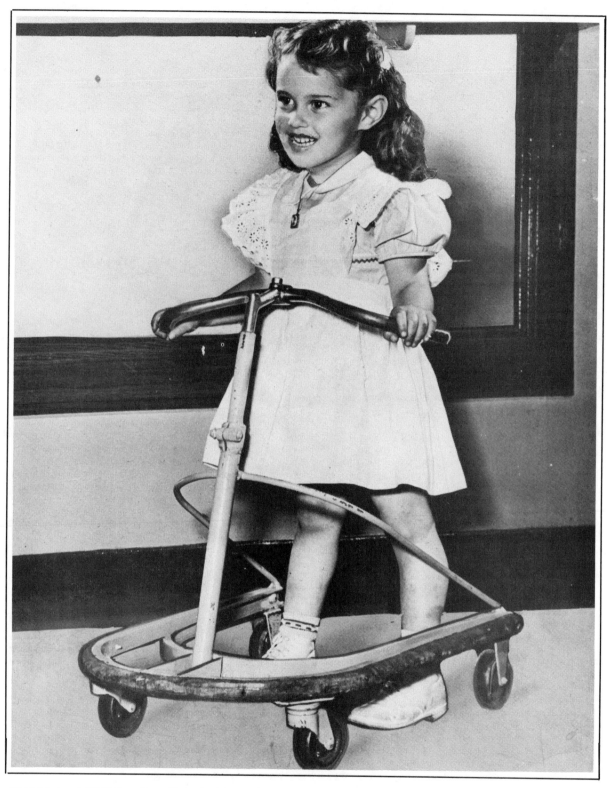

*1949 National Child Bette Jean Bligh, disability at birth, age 4.*

*1950 National Child Russell Miller, age 6, cerebral palsy.*

*1951 National Child Brett Downes, age 4, cerebral palsy.*

*1952 National Child Doris Desrosiers, age 5, cerebral palsy.*

*1953 National Child Freddie Wilson, age 9, cerebral palsy.*

*1954 National Child Karen Albrecht, age 5, cerebral palsy.*

*1955 National Child Billy Jennings, age 6, paraplegic.*

*1956 National Child Clara Jo Proudfoot, age 4, spina bifida.*

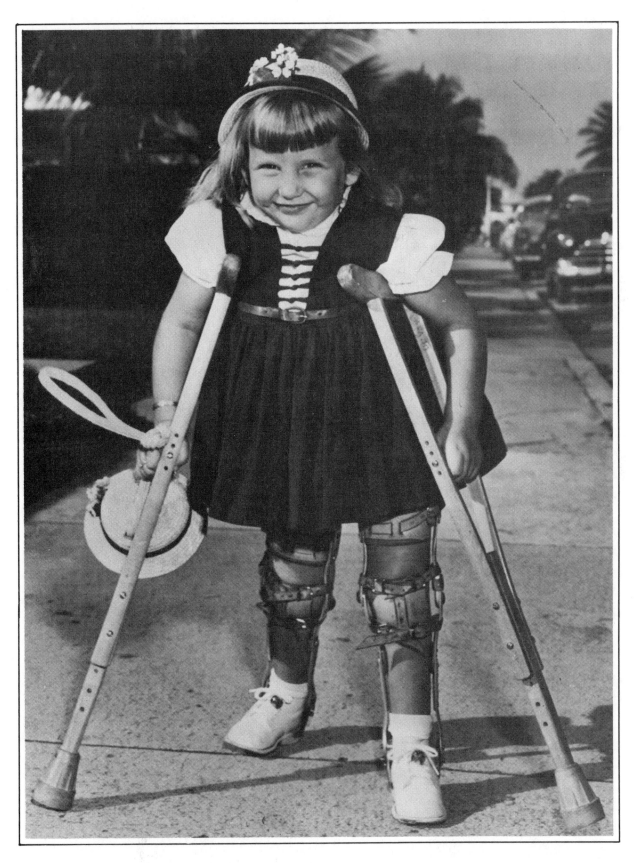

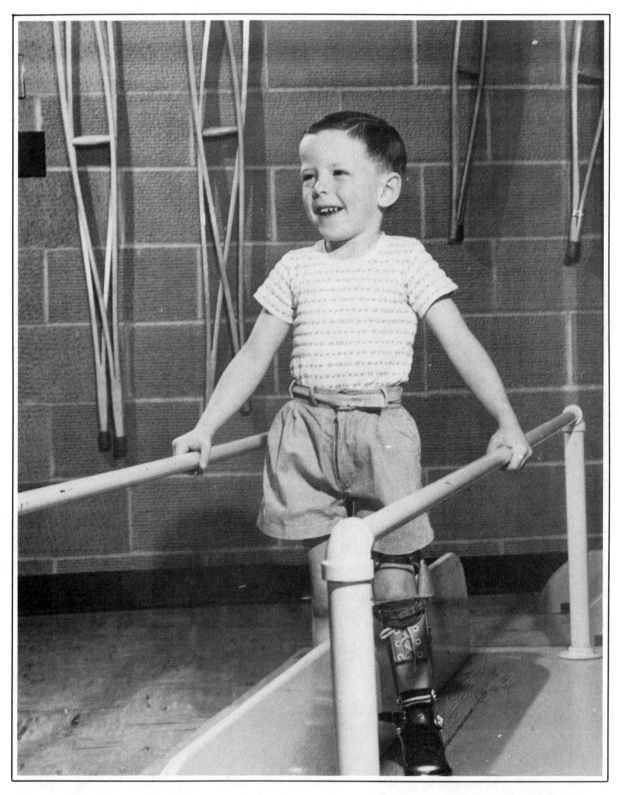

*1957 National Child Walter Bill Cash, age 5,*
*poliomyelitis.*

*1958 National Child Mary Lynne Dunnuck, age 6,*
*cerebral palsy.*

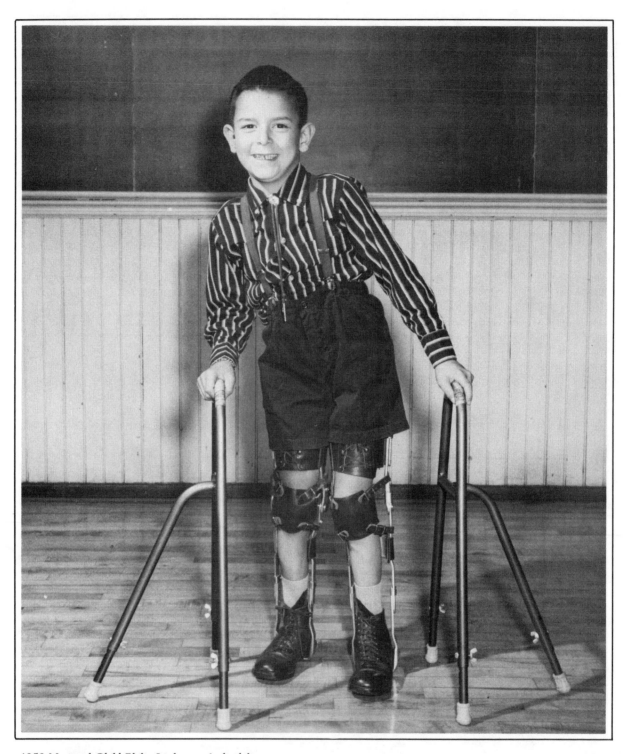

*1959 National Child Philip Little, age 6, disability at
birth.*

*1960 National Child John Kemp, age 10, congenital amputee.*

*1961 National Children Patricia and Paula Webber, age
8, cerebral palsy.*

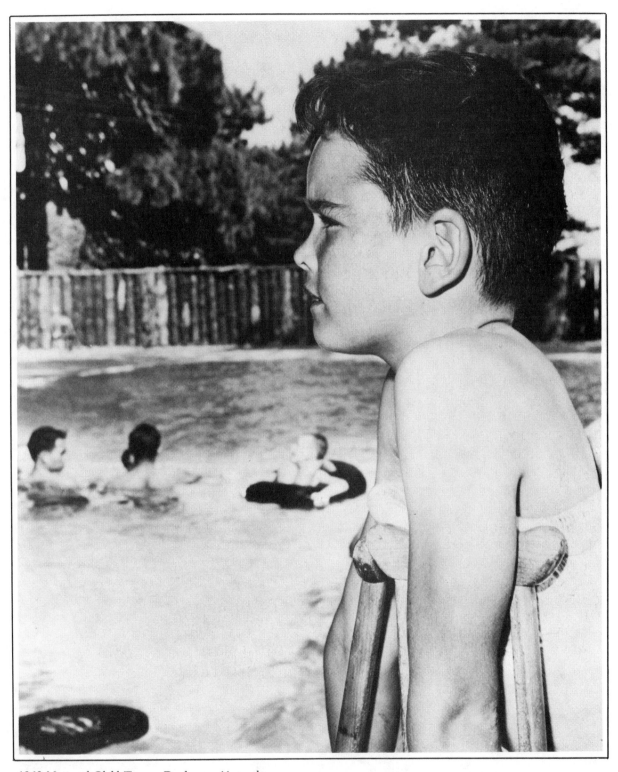

*1962 National Child Tommy Doyle, age 11, perthes.*

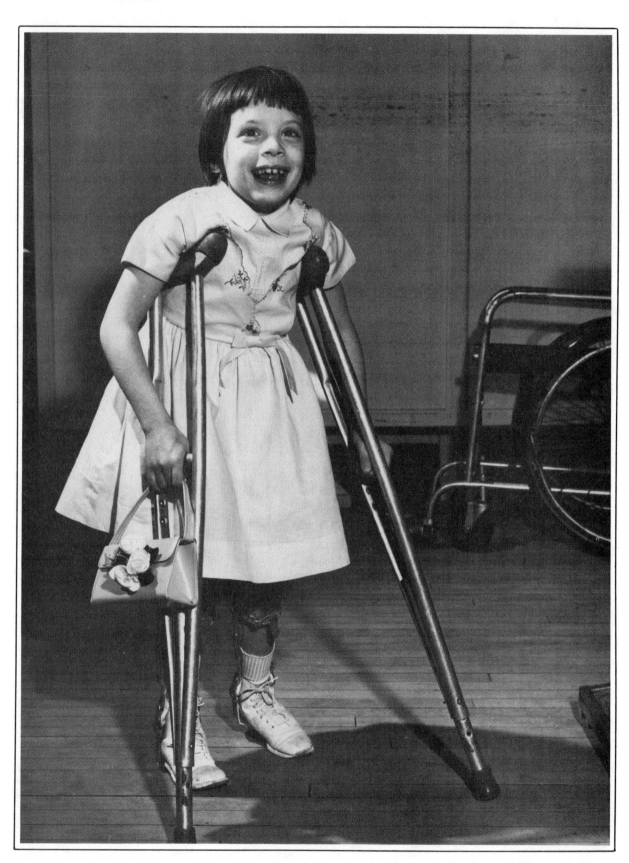

1964 National Children Ronnie and Donnie Cooper, age
6, cerebral palsy.

1963 National Child Brenda Heaton, age 8, cerebral
palsy.

*1965 National Child Donna Staten, age 10, survivor of
a fire.*

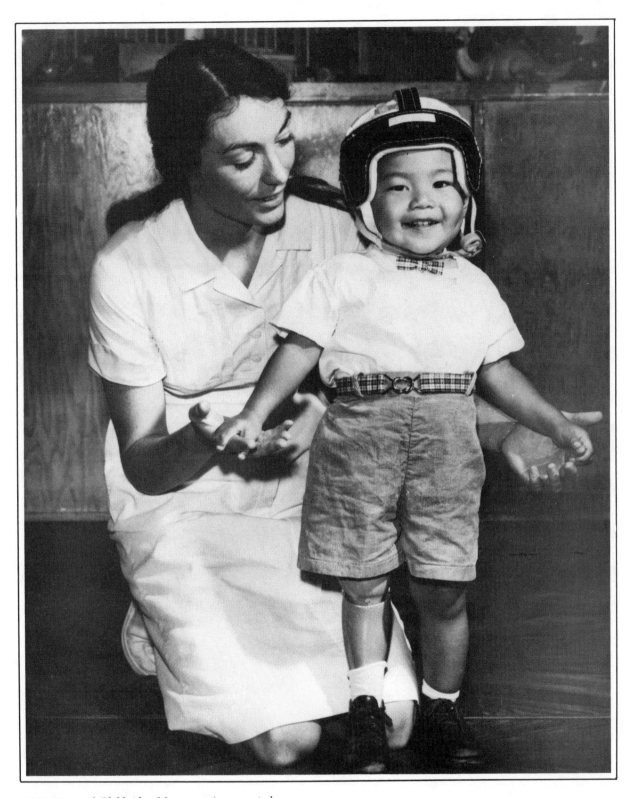

*1966 National Child Alan Ngao, age 4, congenital amputee.*

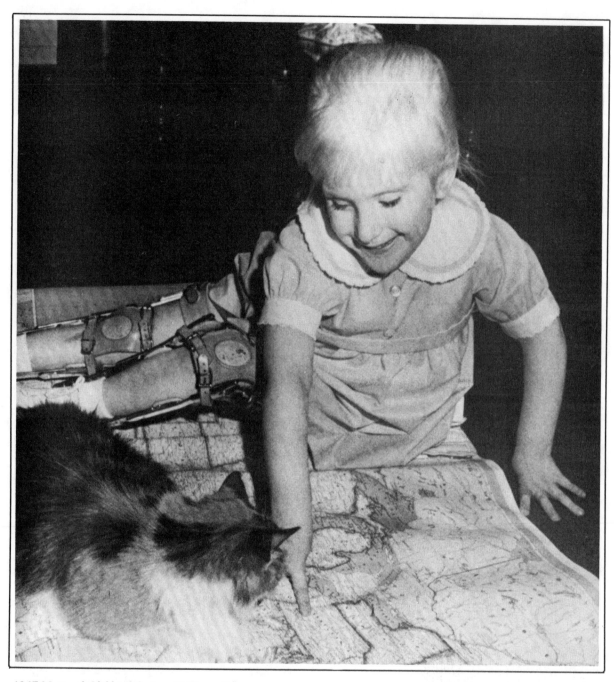

*1967 National Child Leigh Ann Huff, age 5, spina bifida.*

*1968 National Children Lisa and Lori Yauch, age 4,
cerebral palsy.*

*1969 National Child Donna Kay Howell, age 7,*
*childhood stroke.*

*1970 National Child Lori Jean Bowen, age 3, spina bifida.*

*1971 National Child Peter Heltemes, age 7, cerebral palsy.*

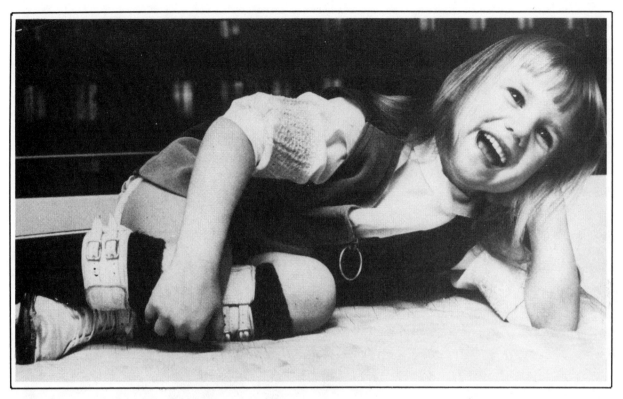

*1972 National Child Jo Anne Schaffer, age 4, cerebral palsy.*

*1974 National Child Tammy Bryant, age 7, auto accident survivor.*

*1975 National Child Pamela Jo Baker, age 5, cerebral palsy.*

*1976 National Child Kerri Hines, age 5, cerebral palsy.*

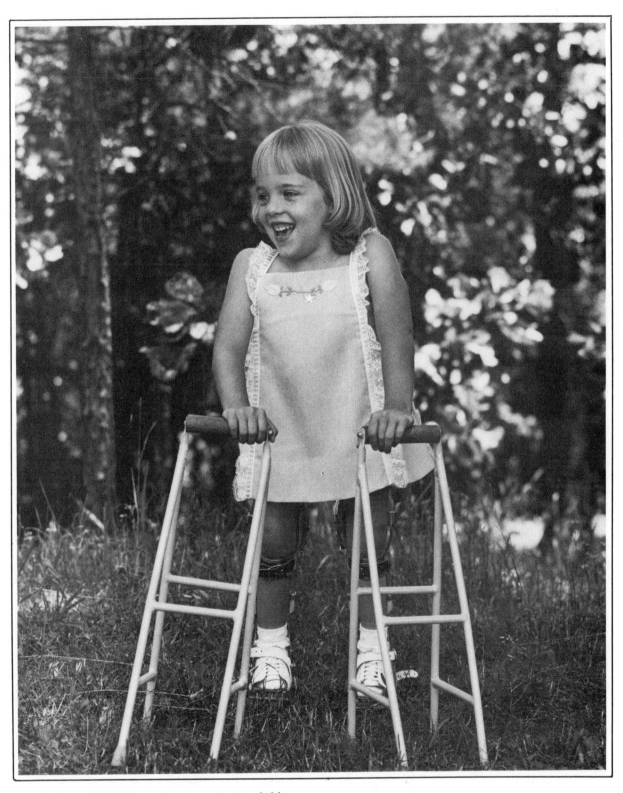

*1977 National Child Danya Steele, age 7, spina bifida.*

*1978 National Child Tony Zidek, age 6, spina bifida.*

# HI! I'M CLAIRE HUCKEL

**SEVEN-YEAR-OLD PHILADELPHIA MISS IS 1979 NATIONAL EASTER SEAL CHILD**

How do you describe Claire Huckel, 7, of suburban Philadelphia, the National Easter Seal Child for 1979? Pretty and cute? Sugar and spice and everything nice? Handicapped? Claire is partially handicapped due to cerebral palsy. She is still pretty and nice, able to enjoy childhood to the fullest, and is a living testimonial of the value of early diagnosis and treatment of a disabling condition. At age two, Claire was enrolled in the Bucks County Easter Seal Center, Levittown, Pennsylvania, to begin a program of therapy and speech and language stimulation. After attending the Easter Seal pre-school for three years, she attended regular kindergarten. Today, she is a first-grader in the Pen Ryn School, Cornwells Heights. As the National Easter Seal Child, Claire is representative of the many thousands of children and adults helped by the nationwide Easter Seal rehabilitation network.

Claire is a happy child, doing most of the things a seven-year-old likes to do. She helps her mother with meal preparations and helps care for brother Charles, 5. She is learning to swim and shares the family interest in sports. She loves to act and sing and has performed in school plays. Claire has been taking dancing lessons and has appeared in recitals with her class.

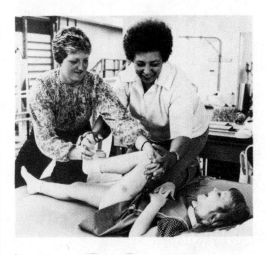

Claire's mother has played an important role in the youngster's therapy program. While Easter Seal therapists work with Claire at the treatment center, Mrs. Charles Huckel, under their guidance, works at home to keep her daughter's coordination and muscular strength as efficient as possible.

## 1979 EASTER SEAL CAMPAIGN
## MARCH 1 - APRIL 15

**THE NATIONAL EASTER SEAL SOCIETY
FOR CRIPPLED CHILDREN AND ADULTS**
2023 W. Ogden Ave., Chicago, Il 60612

*1979 National Child Claire Huckel, age 7, cerebral palsy.*

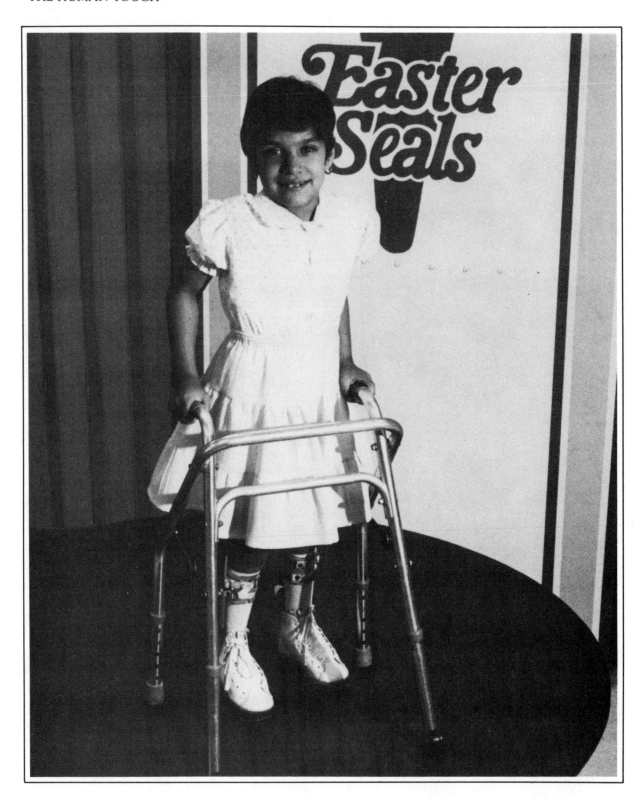

And of course, I continue to be a part of those lives, as time and circumstance allow. We write back and forth, the kids, their parents and I. Just looking through the letters shows me a lot about their growth from kids into young people, from fairly dependent to independent young citizens. They've been wonderful about writing me, sending cards at Christmas and on birthdays, and with my secretary Maureen's help, I've tried never to let a letter go unanswered and have initiated a good many correspondences myself.

Several years ago, I asked Easter Seals to host a reunion of all the kids I'd worked with on my previous telethons. I thought it would be a terrific thing for the telethon audience and I wanted to see my old campaign friends

myself. But additionally, I felt it would reinforce the fact that Easter Seals stays with these individual people long after they are no longer visible representatives.

When we did bring them all back for the big telethon finale, H.B. Barnum led the Life Choir and orchestra as we sang, "That's What Friends Are For." It was far and away the most moving, and meaningful, finale to a telethon I've ever witnessed or been part of.

Each National Child I've worked with and their parents have been asked to reminisce about their most significant memories of the Easter Seal campaign activities. Their responses show why I am so emotionally attached to these people and why I love them the way I do.

*1980 National Child Jeanette Alvarado, age 8, spina bifida.*

Mrs. Finn:

*Easter Seals gave us direction in Colleen's early development. It helped us to know what we could expect with her progress in anything that didn't involve her disability, such as her upper body development, and her large and small motor development and her muscle tone.*

*Because Connecticut law says the school system is responsible for disabled children starting at 33 months, we mostly went to Easter Seals for resource-type people. Easter Seals also worked and communicated with our school system about Colleen.*

*Colleen is 14 now, a freshman in high school. She was only five when she was the 1981 National Child, and doesn't remember everything that happened.*

*One of my favorite memories of her year as the National Easter Seal Child is from the Century 21 convention in Las Vegas. We went to a cocktail party in one of the suites. John Kemp and Pat Boone were there along with a lot of the executives from Century 21.*

*Colleen found the whole thing extremely boring, so she asked Pat to play hide and seek with her. She went and hid—in her wheelchair—behind the curtains and Pat went right along with the game, pretending to look all over for her before, at last, he found her.*

*Another image I will always remember from that convention was 5,000 Century 21 employees all wearing gold suits—all in the same room—and Colleen going up on the stage and whistling for the first time in public.*

*Colleen calls Mr. Boone "Uncle Pat." She didn't realize who he was until just recently. Now she's heard some of his old songs.*

Colleen Finn:

*I'm a freshman now at Shetland High School in Connecticut.*

*Right now I'm most proud of being able to walk with crutches several times a week during certain periods at school.*

*Walking is very important to me.*

*Aside from that, I'm really busy with school and homework and studying. I read a lot, and I like reading books that are in a series, like THE BABY SITTERS CLUB and THE BOXCAR CHILDREN.*

*I'd like to be a teacher when I'm out of school, but definitely one for younger kids. I think big kids, like high school kids, can give a teacher too much trouble.*

Colleen Finn is now 14. She was National Child in 1981.

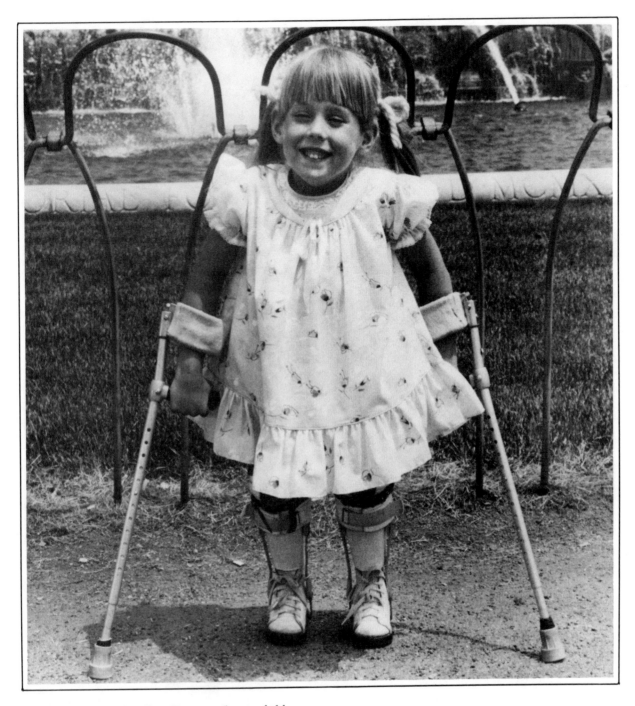

*1981 National Child Colleen Finn, age 5, spina bifida.*

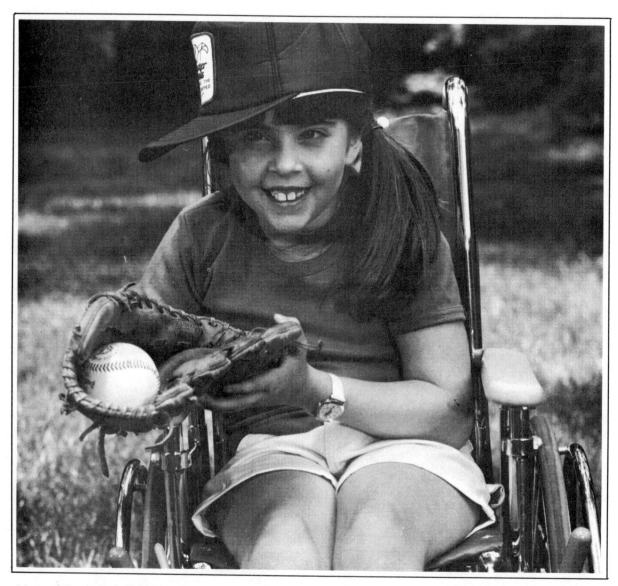

*National Easter Seal Child Mary Sacco, age 7, multiple disabilities.*

### Mrs. Anne Sacco:

*Just after Mary was selected to be the poster child she had an operation in which her shin bone was fused into her ankles. She had to wear casts on both legs for a while afterwards and this made her quite heavy to carry around as we were traveling and things, but everyone was so helpful, giving us a hand whenever we needed it.*

*Then, at the end of her year as National Child, she went to the hospital with a blood clot—a hematoma—on the left side of her brain. She had surgery in September and in three weeks was on her way to Arizona for the Easter Seals convention.*

*It was a miracle she was alive. They had had to burrow a hole to drain the skull. But for Mary it was really downhill from then until Christmas.*

*She felt better after that and enjoyed being the National Easter Seal Child. Mary loved the traveling involved with that role and would travel forever and a day if she could. She has quite a fabulous memory and remembers almost everything from that year even though it was a while ago now and she was rather young.*

*At the telethon, for example, she asked if she could introduce Pat Boone. They wanted her to use cue cards but she wasn't able to read them—so she memorized the whole introduction! She didn't fumble a bit when she gave it and everyone was flabbergasted.*

*She is also quite the one for saying the most unex-*

pected things. When she was National Child, for example, we'd all think she was tuned out or daydreaming and then she'd come up with a really appropriate comment that showed she had actually been listening to every word being said.

She's also a bit of a tease. Before the telethon Rich Little asked her if he should imitate Miss Piggy or Kermit the Frog. Mary picked Kermit. But when he then asked her the same question on stage, she said, "Do Miss Piggy." He was shocked, and Pat thought it was quite hilarious because he knew that wasn't what they had planned.

Mary doesn't hesitate to speak up for herself. When we were at the White House, the Reagans were chatting with Mr. Boone for a few moments and weren't saying anything directly to Mary. So she just said, "Hey, what about me?" And Nancy Reagan responded, "You're right, Mary, we mustn't neglect you."

And on the telethon, Mary said, "I want to thank all of you but I still do need a little more help."

When Mary ended her year as National Child and was sick we heard from everyone we had met through Easter Seals. So many people got in touch with her and kept her in their prayers! We got cards and calls from all over the country. We all needed a boost then, and we got it!

She had four more brain operations that year and finally her condition was stabilized. Actually, the whole situation ended up causing her more motor damage, but it improved her mentality—I guess because all that pressure was off her brain.

Pat kept in touch with her the whole time she was sick and kept her in his prayers.

Pat is a great human being to do what he does. He's busy with so many other things yet he always finds time for Easter Seals. He puts in a lot of hard work, and he's an excellent guy to keep it up.

Mary's written to him several times, and she's always gotten a reply from him.

She also really enjoyed the five-year telethon reunion with Pat. All the children spoke and she did a beautiful interview. It was so natural for her. We all had one great time.

The other people who meant a lot to us during Mary's year as poster child were Gloria Cook, who was president of the Easter Seal board at the time and who has remained a close friend of Mary's, and Jerry McCoy, a fighter from New York. Jerry even flew to Arizona to see Mary after her operation and he said, "We're both fighters and you're going to win this one."

Easter Seals has helped a great deal with Mary's mental and physical development. The therapists worked on her memory, speech and understanding as well as her muscular coordination. She made unbelievable gains in just three years after she started going to Easter Seals.

When Mary first began the Easter Seal swim program she was three years old and stiff as a board. Now her mobility in the pool is unbelievable. She says I'm the handicapped one in the water—and she's right! Mary is 16 now, and she still swims year round. The exercise is great for her.

I actually think being busy with all the poster child activities helped Mary heal faster. She's a strong child, she would have to be to have gone through so much and still be here.

All the National Easter Seal Child Representatives have been through a lot.

Raising Mary is still a full-time commitment. Her memory is great, but she is still working on independent living skills.

Mary's been lucky in many ways—not that she was born with so many problems, but that she's been able to get the help and care she's gotten.

Mary is the light of our life. I don't know what we'd do without her.

Mary Sacco is now 16. She was 8 when she served as National Child in 1982.

I really like to sing. I remeber when Pat Boone and I did a couple of songs together on the telethon—"A Pocketful of Hope" and "The Rose." The other kids sang with him too and we had a lot of fun.

I also remember when I fooled Rich Little. Before the telethon he asked me if I wanted him to imitate Miss Piggy or Kermit the Frog, and I said Kermit.

But when he asked me that out on stage, I said, "Miss Piggy." He looked real surprised and Pat Boone was laughing because he knew we had planned to do Kermit and now Rich Little had to think back real fast for how to do Miss Piggy instead. It was pretty funny!

I also liked introducing Pat Boone on the telethon. He was amazed when I could remember everything I was supposed to say without even reading any of it from the cards.

The telethon was fun. I even answered the phones for a while when people called in to pledge.

I've met a lot of nice people through Easter Seals. And I still participate in the Easter Seal swim program.

## Mrs. Carol Huston:

*We were a bit short on family when Matt became the National Easter Seal Child, and we were having kind of a tough time. But the people at ES really came through for us. They were extremely nice and helpful and became kind of a second family for us.*

*It was a long year that year (actually the National Child appearances went on for about a year and a half) but we really enjoyed it. We traveled coast to coast, and even went to Toronto for the Ramada convention and to Hawaii for the Century 21 convention.*

*Matt had a great time as a poster child—traveling, riding in limousines and staying in suites (not just rooms!) at the Ramada Inns. He thought it was all quite luxurious.*

*Limo drivers would show up at the airport with cards saying "Matt Huston" and Matt would say "Mom, that's me!" It made him feel very special.*

*We also got to fly first class as the guests of Eastern Airlines. Matt was stunned the first time a stewardess put a little tablecloth down in front of him for his meal.*

*On that same flight the pilot announced that Matt was on the flight, and everyone in the plane applauded.*

*Matt also loved meeting all the clebrities—especially Lorne Greene and Tom Selleck.*

*Greene was the luncheon speaker at the Ramada convention. When he walked in I said "It's Pa Cartwright!" and Matt said "Commander Adama!"*

*Greene said, "Talk about a generation gap!"*

*On another trip Matt was given a key to Tampa, Florida, and a free trip to Disney World and Sea World.*

*He visited Shamu's tank and suddenly, out of nowhere, Shamu popped right up out of the water, right next to Matt and the trainer, and he was HUGE up close like that. I thought Shamu was going to eat both of them right on the spot. The trainer eventually got Matt to pet Shamu—very, very tentatively.*

*When we visited the White House, Matt just couldn't believe it when the marine on guard saluted HIM. The marine remained at rigid attention, but Matt kind of sidled up close to him and the marine snuck his hand down and held Matt's hand while we waited to get in.*

*Matt also fell madly in love with Debby Boone— all the Boone sisters, really, but Debby most of all. Once he got a hold of her hand and wouldn't let go. He just closed his eyes and said, "I'm in Heaven."*

*At the telethon all four Boone sisters, three in person and one from Seattle, sang "The Rose" to Matt. He didn't know which one to look at next.*

*Matt really enjoyed the reunion Pat had with the first five National Easter Seal Child Representatives he did the telethon with. Usually the kids just get to meet the child just before and after their year, so this was a nice opportunity for him to meet some of the others.*

*Matt was 10 when he was National Easter Seal Child and he's 16 now. He's a junior in our regular local high school. He's real healthy, and real smart.*

## Matt Huston:

*Meeting the president when I was National Child really sticks in my mind. We were held in a big secretary's room until it was time for us to go in. I remember looking around at all the valuable stuff in there, like all the vases—"vahses," I should probably say.*

*Then someone came and led us down this long hallway to the president's office. We went in and there he was, sitting behind this big desk which had a lot of pictures on it.*

*It was kind of scary to meet him, but not too much. He said a lot of presidential stuff, kind of official sounding talk, you know. And he gave me an apothecary jar full of presidential jelly beans.*

*I wasn't allowed to eat the jelly beans, but his secretary had put some other jelly beans into a little bag and slipped them to me when no one was looking. Those I ate, and they were just regular old jelly beans, but they were good.*

*I still have the jar of jelly beans, but now they're all kind of sticking to the sides of the jar.*

*I gave President Reagan some pencils with the name of my school on them. I figure he probably used them to sign some important treaty or something.*

*Later he sent me some autographed pictures.*

*Another thing I liked about being National Child was riding in all those limousines. They were really long and fancy and most of them had TVs!*

*At the time there was a TV show with the main character named Matt Houston—but spelled the wrong way. The character was played by Lee Horsley. When I met him on the Easter Seal Telethon, he gave me a jacket that said from Matt Houston—spelled his incorrect way—to Matt Huston, spelled my right way.*

*I also remember sitting in Tom Selleck's red Ferrari convertible. I played with the radio and made the antenna go up and down. I also got to watch him tape*

*1983 National Child Matt Huston, age 10, transverse myelitis.*

his show. He really messed up a lot—they had to rehearse the same scene over five times! Tom looked over his shoulder to me and joked, "See, Matt, they still pay me even though I make mistakes."

I also met Tom Selleck's bodyguard. He was definitely the bodyguard type—about eight feet tall. But he was real nice too.

Right now I'm mostly into schooling. I'm also working writing a book—an adventure kind of book. I've got the beginning and the end. Now I just have to work on the middle.

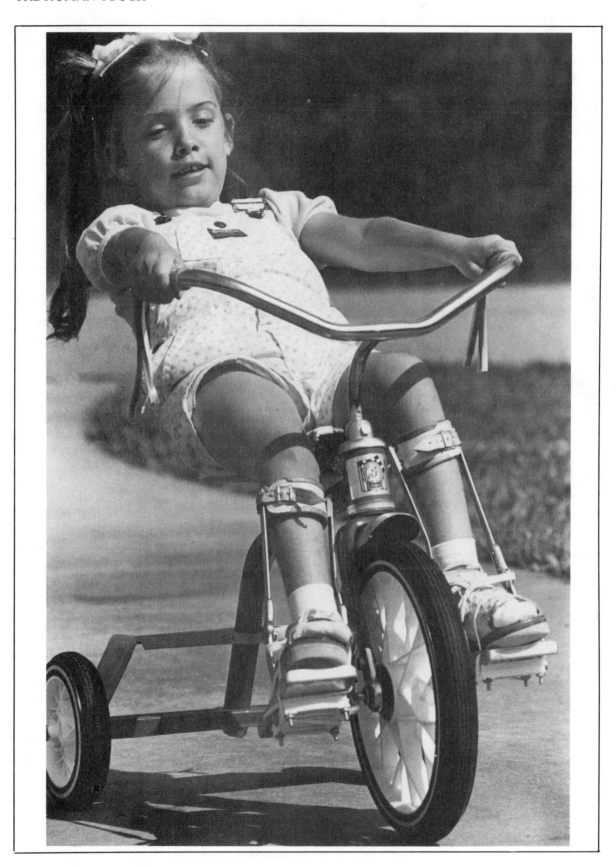

Mrs. Carla Swiney:

*Pat, who's from the South himself, called Stephanie and me "the Southern Belles."*

*At the convention in Las Vegas, Pat introduced Stephanie and said, "I know you must love grits!" Actually, she hates grits, but she decided she'd better not tell him that was the case.*

*Right after the telethon in '84, Stephanie was put into a body jacket to keep her body aligned correctly. She's been in it ever since, but soon will have some major surgery. If it's successful, she'll be out of the body jacket and back to just leg braces and crutches. The two surgeries entail a spinal fusion, the removal of some discs and the putting in of Harrington rods.*

*Stephanie has always had a lovely voice. She's been singing since she was two, and the first thing she did when she met Mr. Boone was say, "I have a song I want to teach you, Mr. Boone."*

*It was "Neglect Not the Gift," written by her aunt especially for Stephanie.*

*I also remember that at the '86 telethon reunion of all the poster children Pat had worked with from 1981 to 1985, Pat said to Stephanie, "I hear you've been doing a lot of walking."*

*Stephanie had been working her way around a track at school that was probably about a quarter mile. He asked her how far she'd been walking and with her 10-year-old sense of distance at the time said "about three feet." She had no idea how to measure the distance she'd been walking, but when she said "three feet" she thought that was pretty good and she was being really cool!*

*Stephanie is taking voice lessons now, and also studying flute and piano. She sings a lot of Christian songs, especially those by Sandy Patty and Bill Gaither, such as "In Heaven's Eyes."*

*She's 13 now and in 8th grade. She's in the marching band at school. She has a uniform and her dad pushes her along in her wheelchair as she plays her flute. She usually walks with crutches and braces, but that doesn't work very well with the marching band.*

*It might seem difficult for some to understand the following statement: The past almost fourteen years have been years of joy, discouragement, renewal of strength, blessings, fears and learning to trust. These are years that I would not trade for anything.*

*When Stephanie was a baby, I did not know physically what lay ahead for her. However, I did know*

1984 National Easter Seal Child Stephanie Swiney, age 8, spina bifida.

*that strength of character, determination, a sense of self worth, a faith that God is in control would determine her ability to deal with her disability.*

*My goal for her was to see her face her life with a sense of challenge and determination. I wanted her to learn to be an independent person but never ashamed to ask for help when needed.*

*We've shared many tears of joy, victory, discouragement, encouragement. Each of us has grown as an individual. I've seen my children develop a sensitivity to the pain and trials of others and to respond to those needs.*

*The long hours of commitment have rendered their rewards. Before me I am seeing my determined little girl develop into a lovely young lady. The eighteen operations and the hard work have been tough taskmasters, but valuable teachers in the development of this young lady as well as her family.*

*My prayer is that each day as we meet other people whether they have disabilities or not that we look beyond the physical body and really see that person who resides inside.*

Stephanie Swiney:

*I remember when I was National Child and we were sitting in the hotel lobby waiting for Mr. Boone to get in from the airport. We were all going to go out to dinner—my family, Mr. Boone and some Easter Seals people.*

*We had told my little sister, Tre, who was four at the time, that Mr. Boone always wore white shoes.*

*Well, when he came walking into that lobby he didn't have white shoes on. I didn't know if Tre noticed or not because she didn't say anything at the time, but then the three of us (Tre, Mr. Boone and I) were riding to dinner together in the same car and Tre looked down and said, "Mr. Pat Boone, you have to wear your white shoes to the White House tomorrow." And he did.*

*When I met President Reagan he told me a story about his desk, which he said was made out of an old boat. He was really nice, but his desk looked like just a regular desk to me.*

*The president also gave me a jar of "presidential jelly beans," with an embossed presidential seal. I've never opened that jar of jelly beans—I don't want to break the seal!*

*I also remember something funny that happened at the telethon. The Ralston Purina Company was giving me a golden retriever named Sunshine. She was* a year and a half old at the time.

The man from Ralston Purina wanted to present her to me during the telethon. So first they showed a video of her, and then the Ralston Purina man went to get her and bring her onstage. He began scratching Sunshine's head until she was totally relaxed. When the camera went to her, she was lying on her back and just wouldn't get up. The entire nation saw the trained guide dog with her legs up and tummy shining!

Mr. Boone said, "Just relax, Sunshine." And she did.

I still have Sunshine. She's six and a half now, and a real good dog. I brought her to school for pet day.

The other thing I remember about being a poster child is actually something I hardly remember at all.

We went out for dinner with Mr. Boone one night after we'd been shooting pictures all day. I was so tired my head just fell over onto the plate before they had even brought any food out. Mr. Boone pushed my stroller back to my hotel room.

What I'm most proud of in my life is having overcome my disability and being able to do anything that I set my mind to.

I've been swimming for nine years and I'm now learning how to play golf and tennis. I like them both.

I like school and I'm a statistician for my school's basketball team. I like math a little, but not too much. I'm also a member of the student government.

I'm thinking about being a teacher in an elementary grade.

I also hope to do lots of work with Easter Seals.

They helped me with my braces when I was younger, and also sent me to Camp Easter in the Pines a couple of summers.

Easter Seals is very important to me. Through my national year, my family and I were able to share with many people the importance of developing and focusing on your abilities rather than your limitations.

Stephanie Swiney was National Child in 1984, at age 8. She is 16 today.

---

Mrs. Diane Sibley:

When Danielle was little, Easter Seals was always there for us, on the parent level as well as the child level. When we went to Easter Seals, Danielle would go to her therapy sessions while I attended group support sessions with a social worker and other parents of children receiving Easter Seal therapy. These sessions really helped me keep going on. I was a single parent at the time and especially appreciated all the support I got in them. Those sessions are important to anyone who has a young child with a disability. I miss those sessions now. They were a very important part of growing up with Danielle, who started at Easter Seals when she was about one-year old.

I'm happy I was able to be a national parent with Danielle, and able to tell other people out there whose children have disabilities that things will eventually get better. Lots of people don't have a base to touch when someone in their family has a disability, or they don't know that Easter Seals is out there. They're one of thousands of people dealing with disabilities, but they don't know it until they come into contact with Easter Seals.

Being the National Child and mother was a lot of work, but we had such a tremendous year. It was the chance of a lifetime to meet all those people, not just the actors but also the corporate sponsors who are so committed to helping people. It's quite admirable in this day and age that the corporate sponsors work so hard to raise money for Easter Seals just because they want to and for no other reason.

Danielle made some lasting friendships during her year as poster child. For example, Rob Weller just called her last week, even though he didn't even know she had been in the hospital. It really perked her up to know he still thought about her. He's kept in contact with Danielle since she's been about three, when she met him through our local Easter Seals fundraising events.

With Danielle's disability, spina bifida, she will continue to need surgery throughout her adolescent growth period and possibly somewhat thereafter. So, in addition to dealing with normal adolescent adjustments to junior high and other things, Danielle has also been dealing with extended periods of hospitalization. Going to the hospital now is a different experience for her than when she was young, so we have to handle things differently, as parents do whenever their children get older. Danielle knows what pain is now, she knows what they will do to her and she knows that when she wakes up from the surgery she will be

*1985 National Child Danielle Newman, age 7, spina bifida.*

in some pain. *Life is changing for us and for Danielle, and it's not necessarily easier, just different. But we have positive attitudes and that keeps us going.*

### Danielle (Newman) Sibley:

*I really liked traveling to all the different states when I was the National Child and I thought it was a lot of fun to be a celebrity. I remember Pat Boone and Donna Mills and Rob Weller, who was one of my favorites. We did a lot of photo sessions together and really everything was a lot of fun.*

*I enjoyed meeting President Reagan too. He gave me a jar of jelly beans which I've saved as a souvenir. They're probably stale now but it's o.k. because I wasn't planning to eat them anyway.*

*I think the people who met me when I was National*

Child *probably learned they were helping kids like me when they contributed to Easter Seals.*

*I'm twelve now and in seventh grade, although I haven't been in school much this year because I've been in the hospital so much having different surgeries on my back.*

*These days I like playing games like Pictionary, checkers and crossword puzzles. Sometimes I also read, and I especially like "Teen Magazine." I had been playing the flute in the school band before I had to be hospitalized so much this year, so if I want to get back into the band I'm going to have a lot of catching up to do. I also like to do stained glass window hangings. I paint them and give them for presents.*

Danielle was National Child in 1985 when she was 7. She's 12 today.

---

### Mrs. Denise Brazzell:

*I think the thing Jamie talked about most when he was the National Child was the time he got an unexpected and unplanned ride in a CBS news van.*

*We had been at a congressional reception on Capitol Hill and somehow there was a mixup and the van that was supposed to meet us outside the Capitol building didn't show up.*

*We were scheduled to go right on to another meeting and we couldn't take an ordinary cab because a regular car can't accommodate Jamie's electric wheelchair. So two people from Easter Seals who were with us ran up to a CBS News van that was parked nearby and persuaded the people in the van to give Jamie a ride.*

*Before we knew it two technicians were lifting Jamie's wheelchair right into the van, surrounded by all the video equipment. I still don't understand how they ever fit him in at all; there was so much stuff in there.*

*Well, Jamie just loved it and talked about it all the time to his friends and everybody at home. I think he talked more about it than almost any other aspect of that trip to Washington.*

*Not many people realize what it means to rear a disabled child in this society. It's a constant fight to raise your child to be independent and assertive.*

*As the National Child, and family really, you have one year to help people understand that having a dis-*

*ability does not mean you are a victim and does not mean you are something pathetic. That year is your actual chance to stand up and tell that to people.*

*There's a lot of travel and a lot of attitudes that you have to face, but we all feel very positive about the experience, and I know Jamie feels good about what he did.*

*For us it was also a chance to give back something to Easter Seals. It's hard to be on the receiving end all the time. After all the countless hours of therapy we'd been through at Easter Seals it was good for us to learn how it feels to be on the volunteer end of things and to see what those hours are like.*

*Being the National Easter Seal Child was very exciting for Jamie. After all, how many kids get to meet the president or get to go to Hollywood and meet movie and television stars?*

*We focused a lot on the educational aspects of all the traveling we did that year. For example, when we went to Puerto Rico we took photos, traveled inland to see what the real culture was like there and even bought some Puerto Rican candy that Jamie brought back to school. Jamie learned a lot that year, even if he wasn't always in his classroom.*

*I do see attitudes changing rapidly toward people with disabilities, and a large part of the credit for that goes to Easter Seals. I haven't seen any other organization do so much in regard to that. Part of their service is to change attitudes—and in some way*

*1986 National Child Jamie Brazzell, age 9, spinal cord
injury at birth, with Pat Boone.*

*1987 National Child Susie Wilcox, spina bifida, at the
piano.*

*this may be their biggest service.*

*Jamie has learned not only that he matters, but, hey, as a disabled person he matters. He also understands that absolutely nothing is closed to him. Some things may be closed physically, but nothing is closed to him totally. He might not be able to play football, for example, but there's no reason he couldn't be a football commentator if that's what he wanted to do.*

*He's learned at a young age that nothing is black and white, that there's a gray area concerning most things and that's where people function. I think that's a pretty good thing for anyone to understand.*

*It takes a lot of emotional energy to raise a child with disabilities. Part of my job is to raise Jamie to have enough authority to deal appropriately with the people he will have to hire for the care he needs. I don't want him in a rest home when he is 21. I want him on his own, which means he will have to have someone to help out with certain things. But I don't want him to feel that he has to be grateful to his caregiver. I want him to understand that he is in charge and whoever he hires is his employee.*

*I think we all have to come to terms with the fact that there are going to be more and more disabled people, and that as a society we need to learn how to deal with this. Right now it's the burden of the disabled to make non-disabled people feel at ease with them. Even Jamie as a child realizes this. But the disabled shouldn't have to work so hard in this way. We should learn to be at ease with the disabled.*

Jamie Brazzell is now twelve. He was nine in 1986 as National Child.

*Besides riding in the news van, meeting President Reagan really sticks out in my mind from when I was the National Easter Seal Child. I thought his office looked really nice. It was kind of fancy and elegant, the kind of place I would like to work in myself.*

*So I decided to tell the president that I wanted his job, and he said, "Some days you could have it."*

*Everybody took a lot of pictures when we were there and the president gave me a jar of presidential jelly beans—which my mom won't let me eat.*

*The president was nice, but he was shorter in person than he looked on TV. Nancy was there too, and she looked even thinner in person than she did on TV. I also got to meet the president's dog, Rex. He was a nice dog.*

*I'm not exactly sure what I want to do when I'm older, but right now I think I might like to be either an airplane designer or a plane navigator.*

*There are two other things I'd like to say.*

*To people without disabilities, I want to say, Don't be prejudiced against people with disabilities. These are normal people, just like you.*

*And to people with disabilities, I want to say, You can make it in the world and do anything you want if you try hard enough and hang tough.*

---

Mrs. Louise Wilcox:

*After we met President Reagan we went out to dinner with Pat in a D.C. restaurant. While we were waiting in the lobby for our private dining room to be ready, Susie started singing one of Pat's old songs—"Speedy Gonzales" (we had gotten tapes of his songs and I think Susie learned them all—words and melody). She was singing and kind of looking at him to see what his response would be.*

*When he realized what she was doing he joined in and the two of them had a great time just singing together, just entertaining themselves and having a great time. It was the first time they sang together, but not the last.*

*Just before the telethon ended, Susie heard that Pat was going to sing "That's What Friends Are For" for*

*the finale. She asked Pat if she could sing it along with him—totally unrehearsed.*

*He could've said no, but instead he said, "Sure," and they just went out and did it. It was one of the best, most moving finales they've ever had.*

*The words to "That's What Friends Are For" mean a great deal to Susie. She meant and felt what she and Pat were singing.*

*I'm not sure adults always realize how seriously the national kids take what they're doing. Even though they're just children, they understand what they're trying to accomplish as National Child representatives. By the end of the telethon they're usually pretty emotionally involved with the whole thing, and have begun to see it as kind of a mission.*

*There's a lot more to being a National Child than just having a good time.*

Susie Wilcox is now thirteen. She was ten when she served as National Child.

Susie Wilcox:

*I'm in seventh grade now. I'm in a bowling league, and I like to shop, listen to music, go to movies and check out boys. I still like to sing—I'm in the chorus at school.*

*When I was the National Child I used to love Matthew Laboroteux from "Little House on the Prairie." I had watched all the old episodes since I was four and he was one of my favorite stars. I used to think "Wouldn't it be great to meet him?"*

*Well, one day the phone rang and I answered it and it was him! My mother was in the shower and I screamed "Oh my God!" and she came running out of the shower. She took one look at the expression on my face and knew who I was talking to.*

*It was pretty exciting. We talked a long time, about everything—dogs, old episodes of the show, everything. He also talked to my mother and older sister!*

*I met a lot of stars when I was the National Child and they were all really nice to me. I met John Denver, Ricky Schroeder, Joel Higgins, Robert Goulet, Johnny Cash, Roz Ryan, Donna Mills, Katherine Helman and Nell Carter, and some others.*

*My other favorite was Danny Amatullo from "Fame." I used to sleep with a picture of him under my pillow! I met another person from "Fame" and he told him how much I liked Danny Amatullo and he said, "Why not come to the set after I finish lunch and you can meet him?"*

*Well, I got there and there he was, just sitting reading his lines! He kissed me on the cheek twice—once when I got there and once when I left!*

*When I grow up I want to do three different things—first be a cop, then a lawyer, then a judge. I want to be a judge who gives out tough sentences, not wimpy ones, because I think the police have a hard job to do and they need tough judges to support their work and also to make sure the citizens get the protection they need. But I want to start out as a cop first because that way I'll really know what their work is like.*

*I don't want people to ever say I "suffer" from a disability. I HAVE a disability, but I don't suffer from it. I really want people to understand that.*

*People, especially kids, should feel free to ask me why I'm in a wheelchair. To me that's just a healthy outlet, a healthy question. It shows me they want to learn about me.*

*I would also really like to get invited to other kids' houses more often. I want to say to everybody, "Just because I'm in a wheelchair don't be afraid to ask me over. I can get there, and I can get around when I'm there."*

*I'm a person like everyone else and I WANT to be TREATED like everyone else.*

*And I want the words WANT and TREATED in capital letters!*

---

Mrs. Diane Dennsteadt:

*Shawn is 10 now and a funny, typical boy.*

*I remember a photo session he did for New Jersey Easter Seals when he was holding a huge red ripe tomato (the symbol of New Jersey) in one hand and a big apple (the symbol for New York) in the other while sitting on Pat Boone's lap.*

*Pat of course was wearing his perfect white suit, while Shawn was sitting there on his lap kind of tossing the tomato up and down. For the longest time Pat didn't say a word but everyone in the place could feel what he was thinking and Shawn of course knew exactly what he was doing.*

*Finally Pat said "You gonna be careful with that?"*

*and Shawn said "Yep." Luckily, nothing happened with the tomato—or the suit!*

*Shawn also teased Pat a bit at the Century 21 convention in Las Vegas. Pat was speaking behind the podium, and Shawn was in front of it, where Pat couldn't see what he was doing. I had left a glass of water there on the stage, and Shawn kept pretending he was going to drink it or sit on it, that kind of thing, and everyone in the audience was laughing. Pat didn't realize they weren't laughing at what he was saying.*

*Shawn is quite good at imitating people, including President Reagan. When Shawn visited the president as National Child he showed Mr. Reagan how he could do a shoulder stand on a skateboard—right there in the oval office.*

*1988 National Child Shawn Dennsteadt,*
*femur-fibula ulna syndrome, riding his skateboard.*

When he finished he said to the President, "Now it's your turn" and Reagan responded, "When you get to my age you don't do that anymore." Shawn does a great imitation of that line, with a raspy, quivery voice and everything.

Shawn also does a funny imitation of Mike Tyson, whom he met during his year as National Child. He gave Mike a little gift—a little statue of a boy and a dog. Shawn describes how Mike tore open the package and ripped the styrofoam around the statue and then growled, "A boy and a dog? I want a woman!"

Shawn had a great time as National Child, traveling all around and meeting so many people. It was exhausting, but fun.

Easter Seals has made a big difference in Shawn's life and in all of our lives.

They've helped out with his prostheses and helped him get his own computer both at home and at school. They've also helped with his motorized Amigo wheelchair and another lighter weight wheelchair. Shawn can walk but it would be too much for him to get through a whole shopping mall, for example, so he needed this equipment.

People from Easter Seals also negotiated with Shawn's school when the school wanted to place him in a special program. Easter Seals persuaded the school officials to mainstream Shawn into a regular class—including regular gym. He's doing very well in school, including gym, where he has his own way of doing things.

Shawn pushes himself to achieve things—he has an A or B average and he can shoot baskets in gym. The teachers all say they wish the other students tried as much as he does. In fact last year they dedicated the school yearbook to Shawn as its most outstanding person.

He's not treated any differently from any of the other kids at school—or at home for that matter—and is punished like the rest of them when he has to be.

He's a very relaxed kid, and a typical boy. About the only time I heard him complain when he was National Child was when he said his face muscles were hurting from smiling so much.

Shawn Dennsteadt is ten today. He was eight in 1988 when he was National Child.

Shawn Dennsteadt:

I had fun being the National Easter Seal Child. I remember trying to show Pat Boone how to skateboard in a park near his house in California but he kept falling off.

I was a little nervous meeting President Reagan, but it seemed like Pat was a little nervous too. The president was funny—I liked his voice.

When I was skateboarding in the president's office Pat told me I shouldn't stand on my head too long, because all the blood would run into it.

I think my favorite part about being National Child was meeting Mike Tyson. We did a speech together at the telethon and he said, "Thanks for being a friend."

I met a lot of famous people during that year. They were all nice, but I learned that famous people are not any different from regular people.

Easter Seals has done a lot for me, like helping me get my prostheses and my computers. I'm planning on doing more for them too.

Right now I'm mostly just busy being a kid.

---

Mrs. Janet Hall:

The moment I remember most from Joy's year as National Child was when she sang "The Greatest Love of All" at the telethon conference in Las Vegas. Everybody—and I'm talking about several hundred people, including corporate sponsors and telethon people and Easter Seal people—stopped talking and stood up and held hands while they listened to Joy sing. It was such a wonderful, touching moment.

Being the national mom was really quite an experience.

People have a lot of misconceptions about disabilities, but disabilities can happen to anyone.

I've always fought so Joy could live a normal life. No one was going to stop me from doing that—but Easter Seals made it a little easier.

I am beginning to see some changes in attitudes toward people with disabilities. And often I see those changes happen after someone has met Joy. I just wish it could have started earlier.

Joy was the first disabled child in her school. I had to work hard to make the school officials come around to make the school accessible for Joy. There wasn't a

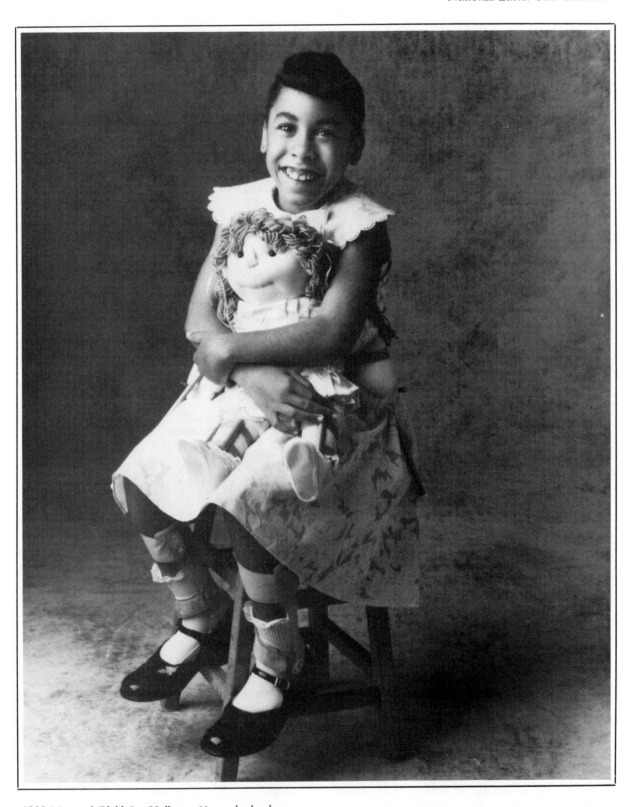

*1989 National Child Joy Hall, age 11, cerebral palsy.*

*ramp, and it took a whole year for one to be put in because the school didn't want to make any changes.*

*I've learned that I have to talk to people, look at them or do whatever else is needed until they come around all right in this kind of thing.*

*There are also many people with a lot of compassion. We got cards and letters from people all over the country when Joy was National Child, and I never expected that. We even got a tape from two people who made up a song about Joy!*

*I'm now on the board of our local Easter Seal Society here in Baltimore, and it's quite fascinating to see how everything works from this point of view. I understand now where the money goes and how it's spent. It makes me really appreciate the corporate sponsors and their million-dollar contributions.*

*It's good to see all this come together. I hope more and more people start helping.*

Joy Hall is twelve today. She was National Child in 1989.

Joy Hall:

*My favorite moment as National Child? Goodness gracious, when I sang that song and the whole house rocked! Everybody was standing and holding hands and crying and swaying together as I sang. The only one who wasn't crying was me. I just sang!*

*I was glad I could make them feel like that.*

*It was a lot of fun being the National Child and going from here to there all the time, even though it was a little tiring.*

*I liked doing the telethon and seeing all the entertainers.*

*One of my favorites was Sherman Hemsley, who used to be on "The Jeffersons." He had me come onto his own show, "Amen," and had me sing.*

*People asked me a lot of questions when I was National Child, and a lot of people would say things like "I saw you on TV. It's so nice to meet you!"*

*Sometimes people still recognize me and say, "That's the National Child!" It's kind of fun. I like that!*

*To people without disabilities, I'd like to say, if you see someone with a disability, just go over and say hi. Don't go up to them and stand there and stare 'em down the throat or tease them. Just treat them as if they didn't have a disability, but don't forget that they do, because they might need your help.*

*Most of all, remember you're talking to a person, not a person with a disability.*

*To people with disabilities, don't let yourself feel neglected or slighted or anything like that, because if you do it will make you feel worse.*

*If you think positively you'll be fine and you won't have to worry. Sometimes I even forget I have braces on. Just remember that thinking positive really works. If you think bad, it will work out bad.*

*And another thing—don't let people take advantage of you, like pretending to be your friends and really not being your friends. Look for real friends, not people who really just want to know what famous celebrities you met on your trips. You don't want users like that—you want someone to be your real friend, someone who'll help.*

---

Mr. Louis Vance:

*Easter Seals has really helped with Vanessa's success as a person. Easter Seals got her started. Through the therapy, the support and the knowledge she got from Easter Seals Vanessa was able to get into motion. She learned how to get into and out of her wheelchair, how to get around and so many other things.*

*The people at Easter Seals—the therapists, the director, the other parents and children—have become like a second family to us. All the talking we've done there, all the conversations we've had there have given us so much support. And getting to know other people*

*dealing with similar problems has been so helpful.*

*As a result of our involvement through Vanessa, Vivian and I also began doing volunteer work for Easter Seals. We've also both served on the local Easter Seal board.*

*Through Easter Seals we learned about a support group for families of children with spina bifida, which is quite a devastating birth condition in the sense that it causes so many different kinds of problems. The support group has monthly meetings with speakers who discuss the latest information on spina bifida, and that has always been very helpful.*

*Vanessa has had the same therapist now for many years, and what a wonderful, special person she is!*

*1990 National Child Vanessa Vance, age 10, spina bifida.*

She has been a very important factor in everything Vanessa has done, and even now helps, for example, by checking Vanessa's braces for the correct pressure, the right kind of angles.

A lot of the credit for what Vanessa has achieved goes directly to Vanessa herself. She's really done a lot of hard work and has a lot of determination.

I'm thrilled she's been able to be a part of all this as the National Easter Seal Child. She's a good ambassador and it's been a wonderful experience for all of us.

You know, having a child with a disability isn't something you plan on. Until we had Vanessa I didn't really know what Easter Seals was. I would get those stamps in the mail every year and kind of wonder what they were all about.

But now of course we've had the opportunity to go to Easter Seals and the impact has been tremendous.

Vanessa Vance is the 1990 National Easter Seal Child. She turned eleven on Valentine's Day.

Vanessa Vance:

When I first started going to Easter Seals I was only about two so I don't really remember anything that far back. But I do remember when I was about six and the Easter Seals therapist would come to my house and work with me on a lot of different things like walking in between parallel bars, getting up stairs, lifting small weights, standing and also falling the right way. We also did a lot of exercises together.

What I really love now is sports, especially horseback riding. I'd love to have my own farm some day with my own horses and maybe be a famous horseback rider. I also like tennis, basketball, swimming, volleyball, snowskiing and occasionally a little baseball. I tried waterskiing and it wasn't too successful but I do want to try it again.

Lately I've also been getting into wheelchair racing. I've been in two 3.1 mile races in the past six months and my time in the second one was really down from the first one—29.7 minutes, down from 36.35.

One of my goals is to be in the Junior Olympics. I have to wait until I'm 13—that's the minimum age—but I'd like to be in the swimming competition and possibly the wheelchair racing too.

I also like to read whenever I'm bored and don't have anything else to do. I've read 13 Nancy Drew mysteries, a couple of Roald Dahl books, and some of The Babysitters Club books. I also like Judy Blume and Betsy Byars books.

When I grow up, besides being a horseback rider, I think I'd like to be a research scientist and try to figure out ways to prevent birth defects.

I have two messages to give to people.

The first is if you see someone with a disability having difficulty with something, like getting up a curb, wait a bit to see if the person really needs your help or not. And before you give any help, always be sure to ask first. Don't just move someone's wheelchair or grab their arm without asking because if you do it could scare them.

My second message to people is this—pursue what you think is difficult and by love and courage you'll have the power to overcome.

---

Mrs. Patsy Houlihan:

We were thrilled when Bridget was chosen National Child, and look forward to her year. She's someone who will truly enjoy being a spokeperson for other young people with disabilities. Without knowing it, she's been doing this for most of her life.

Tom and I also hope to have the opportunity to talk with other parents of children with disabilities. We'd like to encourage them to find the kinds of experiences that really help parents let go and enjoy their children's growing independence. It's what Easter Seal camping programs helped our family to do.

Bridget has already begun to travel. And she met many of the corporate sponsors and Pat Boone, for the first time, recently. We are all excited about what's to come.

Bridget Houlihan, age 12, from Denver, Colorado, is the 1991 National Easter Seal Child.

Bridget Houlihan:

I'm really looking forward to my year as National Easter

Bridget Houlihan, age 12, cerebral palsy, ready for a day in the mountains.

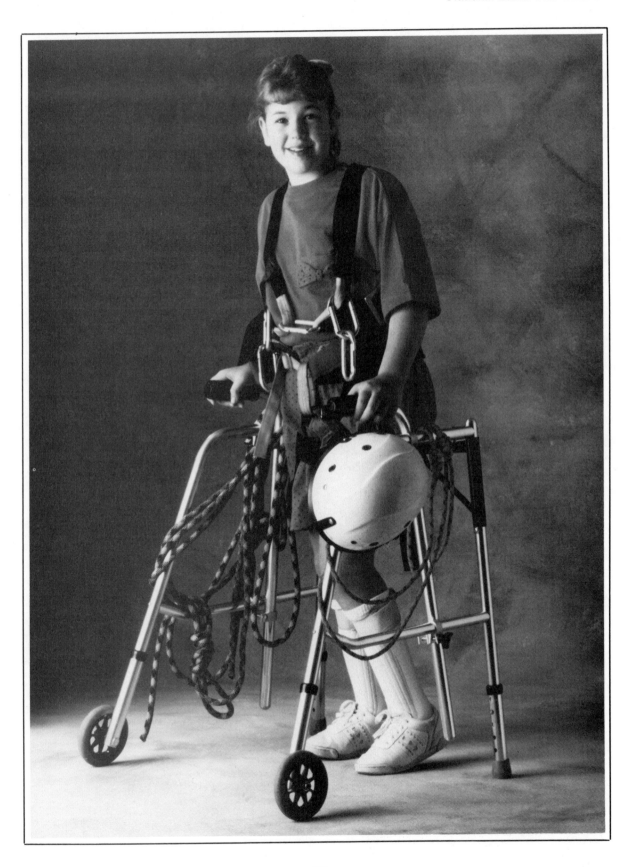

*Seal Child. I've already had the chance to visit Nashville—and "talk Southern"—and Grand Rapids, Michigan, and Los Angeles, where I met Pat Boone, Mary Frann and Robb Weller. I've also been to Chicago three times, once to see the "New Kids on the Block."*

*I hope that I'll have a chance to tell lots of people how important it is to treat people with disabilities like they treat everyone else—as people. I think that I'll be able to explain why it's so important that people with disabilities be considered the same when we look for jobs. I want to be a teacher after I go to college, like my mom, and I hope that I will be considered the same as any other person who wants to teach.*

*The other thing I want to tell people about this year is the Easter Seal camp in the Rockies where I go each summer. I'll bet we've done things that many nondisabled kids haven't done, like traversing rivers on ropes and white-water rafting. My parents say it's given me more confidence and they're right. Taking on a challenge when you're not really sure you can do it, and doing it, is great.*

# VIII
## Easter Seal Adult Representatives

*I*mentioned before, didn't I, that Easter Seals helps people of all ages?

Well, in addition to the ten National Children I've worked with, I have also met several Easter Seal Adult Representatives during my years as telethon host. In 1983 Easter Seals began naming Adult Representatives in addition to National Children to remind the public that it offered services to people of all ages and all disabilities.

I want to underscore this again, and as forcibly as I know how. If I didn't know the scope and range of Easter Seal concern and involvement, even after I'd hosted the telethon a couple of years, I can't expect you to be aware of how far-reaching the programs are. I won't forget my first visit to the Orange County Rehabilitation Center, where I met and spent an afternoon with people who had strokes, as they fought back, with Easter Seals help, to independent living again. And our Adult Representatives help us, often dramatically, in making the larger public aware of the services we do offer and provide.

Each of the Adult Representatives I've met has had a different disability. Some were born with their disabilities, while others acquired their disabilities through illness or accident. All of them have learned how to live independently with some help from Easter Seals.

Let's hear what each of these marvelous people, good friends all, have to say.

Bart Van Housen, 1983–84 Adult Representative from:

*I was born with one of my legs twisted backward and after a childhood filled with multiple surgeries and casts in attempts to correct it I finally had it amputated when I was 22. It was three inches shorter than my other leg and since it had never really been corrected amputation became a preferable choice.*

*I've always been an active person and done as much as I could. In 1982, when I was in my mid-30s, I decided to run from Brookings, Oregon, to Tijuana, Mexico—the length of California—as a fund raiser for Easter Seals.*

*I dedicated the race to Terry Fox, who had then recently died at the age of 21 while attempting to run across Canada to raise money for cancer. He made it three quarters across, running, like myself, with a prosthetic leg—having lost his leg to cancer. I was very affected by his effort and wanted to do something in* his memory as well as to raise funds for a charitable cause.

I had done some research and found that Easter Seals really used its money wisely and offered a lot of different programs for people with disabilities. So I went to them with my idea and they helped provide me with a specially designed prosthetic leg suitable for running. In turn, my run raised about $2 million nationwide, and about $800,000 in the state of California.

I ran about 20 miles a day, almost a marathon a day, for 41 days, taking one day off every six days. There was some controversy at the time about whether this kind of strain was good for me and in all honesty it did cause me some problems. But at the time I was determined to finish the run. My point was not to say to other people with disabilities that they should be doing what I was doing, but to show what a disabled person could do, and maybe to get non-disabled people to think more about their own bodies. I believe that psychological health has a lot to do with physical health.

After my run I was elected to the Easter Seal Sports Council in 1983, 1984 and 1985 and did dozens of other shorter runs—mostly 10 Ks—across the country to raise additional funds for local Easter Seal affiliates. I also ran the San Francisco Marathon in 1982, 1983 and 1986.

I've had a disability all my life and I've found that society generally isn't too excited about people with disabilities. Most of the time people don't even want to think about having a disability unless it happens to them.

In some ways society didn't allow me to participate in it fully until I was older. For example, there were no laws protecting people with disabilities until I was about 30, when Congress passed the federal rehabilitation act of 1977.

I know I've been turned down for jobs because of my disability but right now I'm happy to say that I've had my job as a college registrar for 13 years. I haven't done a marathon for three years but I'm still active and enjoy bike riding, skiing and aerobics. I also swim a mile and a half a day.

I think I do see some attitudes changing a bit regarding people with disabilities. This is encouraging, since society is hard to change. Easter Seals has always been good about trying to re-educate society about people with disabilities. I hope what I did helped.

*1983 Adult Representative Bart Van Housen running with artificial leg.*

# Striving for independence

## For some, it's a very tough fight.

## Back a Fighter

Easter Seals ®
for people with disabilities

## Give to Easter Seals

George Sagona, 1986 National Adult Representative from Apollo Beach, Florida (this was excerpted from Mr. Sagona's campaign materials):

*George Sagona is a man who believes in giving back.*

*He lost a leg in 1982, as a result of diabetes, and felt his life was over. In January 1983, he began a rehabilitation program at the Easter Seal Center in* *Tampa, Florida. Sagona received his artificial leg in March and was discharged in May.*

*Sagona credits the Easter Seal Center and its staff for giving him a new life. He works full-time today, selling for a car dealer near his home in Apollo Beach, Florida. A few years ago, he helped to organize a peer-counseling group called "Amputees Together," which meets periodically at the Easter Seal Center to share experiences and help each other through the adjustments of post-amputation rehabilitation.*

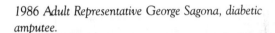

*1986 Adult Representative George Sagona, diabetic amputee.*

Andrew G. Vangelatos, Ph.D., 1987 Adult Representative from Crescent City, California:

*My year with Easter Seals was extremely rewarding. I met many fine people and felt a lot of inspiration from those individuals who contributed so greatly of their time and efforts to further the work of Easter Seals.*

*The most significant event of my year, as the Adult Representative, was when I visited an IBM demonstration. This program showed the latest in computers designed specifically for people with disabilities. It was through this presentation that I found still another way to give back to people with disabilities. I envisioned the establishment of a computer center for people with disabilites, here in Crescent City, California, at College of the Redwoods, Del Norte.*

*When I returned home, I shared my vision with the local chapter of Easter Seals and obtained their financial support of $10,000. This was then matched with $15,000 from the state of California and another $3,000 from Rural Human Services (a local non-profit organization dedicated to assisting people in a variety of ways).*

*With these monies, and additional money from the college budget, we were able to purchase equipment and provide staff for a high-tech center. The educational plan of this center is designed to train disabled people in the use of computers. Ultimately, we hope to qualify these students for the workaday world. Our equipment is state-of-the-art, and it is utilized daily by 30 to 35 students with disabilities. It is one of the best centers of its kind in the state, and I'm very proud of what we've been able to achieve.*

*1987 Adult Representative Andrew Vangelatos, osteomyelitis, playing tennis.*

133

### George Cisneros, Adult Representative:

*After I had my stroke in 1976 and left the hospital my family and I really felt the need for a support group of people who were also dealing with life after a stroke. I went to Easter Seals and said I wanted to start a stroke club, and they agreed to provide space there for us on a weekly basis. In 1977 we started the club, which meets every Thursday, with four people— and now we have 36 who come on a regular basis.*

*Another benefit I have gotten from Easter Seals is the opportunity to go to a trained therapist who discusses my therapy with me and makes sure that what I do I do correctly. It's important for me to be able to discuss this with an expert, because if I were doing my exercises and therapy wrong, they wouldn't do any good and, worse, they could actually be harmful.*

*I'm very active now and I'd really like people to know that having a stroke is not the end of the world, although it may seem so at first. It's really the beginning of a new world, with new challenges and new experiences.*

### Vera Cisneros, George's wife:

*Easter Seals has certainly made a great difference to our family since George had his stroke, particularly in the way the whole family has accepted the stroke and has learned to accept other people who have experienced some kind of trauma like this.*

*George went to Easter Seals for additional therapy after he was released from the rehab center in the hospital and of course he then became involved in starting the stroke club. The club has been so wonderful for us and for all the families who were as lost as we were after someone had had a stroke. The spouses of the club members have formed teams of six or seven and we usually cook a meal for everybody to have after the weekly meeting. As a result we've helped ourselves by discussing what happens when you live with someone who has had a stroke and by asking how they've dealt with all the different things that come up.*

*Easter Seals has been an inspiration and a home for a lot of people. Our experience with Easter Seals has been so enriching. I can't thank them enough for giving my husband the opportunity to use his abilities and giving him a place where he has found new friendships. Easter Seals encourages people to treat people with disabilities just like everyone else. When people don't, it just adds to the problems.*

1988 Adult Representative Col. J. George Cisneros, stroke survivor.

Walt Shinault, 1989 National Adult Representative from Jackson, Mississippi:

*I became paralyzed from the neck down as the result of a freak accident while doing a flip off a mini-trampoline.*

*I remember that night when I was in intensive care and my family was so upset about the whole thing they didn't want to tell me I would be paralyzed from there on out and the doctor didn't want to tell me either so a nurse came in and gave me the news.*

*Needless to say, I was pretty devastated when she told me I had a spinal cord injury and wouldn't be able to move anymore.*

*That night I cried and prayed and eventually realized this was the worst case and I couldn't go down any farther than where I was just then. From that time on I could only go up again.*

*I was already a religious person and I asked God why he let this happen to me and then accepted this as part of his plan somehow.*

*I felt he was saying to me, "Walt, I've ended the first part of your life, but now I'm gonna open up a new one for you." Since then I have felt that I've had two lives, one before and one since my accident.*

*I know God has been with me in my current life because, believe me, there's no way anyone could be strong enough to do any of this without him at your side.*

*I've always been a goal-oriented person and after my accident I set three goals for myself: I wanted get well enough to get back to college, graduate and then get myself a career.*

*Exactly six months to the date after my accident I got out of the rehab center but I had no means of getting myself around and also no insurance.*

*My aunt worked with a woman who was a local Easter Seal representative and she asked if Easter Seals might help me purchase an electric wheelchair.*

*Well, the response was overwhelming. They held two fund raisers for me in my home town of Tunica, Mississippi, under the auspices of Easter Seals.*

*Mine was the only project pending at the time and the town of 92,000 people really came out for me.*

*You know, of course, that 90 percent of what Easter Seals raises stays within the community where it's raised, and 75 percent of that stays within the county.*

*After that Easter Seals also helped reimburse me for the cost of gas for periodic doctor's visits I had to make from Oxford to Jackson, Mississippi.*

*Easter Seals also co-sponsored another fund raiser with a ministerial organization when I needed a computer and a mouth stick for my school work that I now use in my work.*

*Easter Seals was there for me at a critical point in my life. There was no way I could've personally done what they did for me, and had I not gotten that chair at that particular point I probably would've had to go back home to Tunica and missed the opportunities which have kept me going.*

*I graduated from college in 1984 with just enough money for two months' rent. I started to interview for jobs and got a call from Merrill Lynch, where you have to pass a test just to get an interview.*

*I passed their interview test, then passed their hour-and-a-half interview and their three-hour interview, which involves testing applicants to see if they can handle the stress of this kind of work.*

*Merrill Lynch hired me as a financial consultant provided I would get my securities license—another test, and if you fail it, that's it—you can't retake it.*

*Well, I passed that too and now have worked for Merrill Lynch for five years—totally on commission.*

*Like all Merrill Lynch employees, my work performance has been monitored since day 1 to make sure I do a certain percentage of business. I've done just fine, even though there's a forty percent turnover each year of people who don't make it in this business.*

*I've gone around to a lot of corporations and talked about hiring people with disabilities when they're trying to find good quality employees. We've got the minds and the abilities and we really want those jobs. I've been telling these employers it doesn't really matter if we get around or speak somewhat differently from their other employees—we're there to do excellent work for them.*

*The companies I've spoken with have given me a lot of positive feedback and have been using me as an example, saying if he can stay stand the pressure box of working for Merrill Lynch then there must be other people with disabilities out there who could do good work for us.*

*I also go around quite a bit and speak to other people with disabilities. I tell them once they decide what they want to do the world is endless.*

*1989 Adult Representative Walt Shinault, paralyzed from tumbling accident.*

## Mary Lois Stewart (Kay's mother):

Kay was in the special education program in our local public high school and graduated in 1977 when she was 21. We had expected she would attend a special program at a nearby vocational school but that program never materialized.

We didn't know what she would do because she really hadn't learned any job skills in high school and wasn't very mature in the sense of handling the kind of things a job would require.

But, fortunately for us, we heard that Easter Seals in Great Falls had just begun offering a vocational education program for mentally disabled adults. So in the fall of 1977 Kay joined this new program.

Kay had always thought she would go to college. She had never viewed herself as having any limitations at all, so at first attending this program and going from the world of high school to the world of work was a real tough transition time for her. She's very tenacious and stubborn, and at first it was hard to get her to accept that she wouldn't be going to college. But that very tenacity and stubbornness are also the traits that have helped her become as successful as she is today.

Kay did lots of growing at Easter Seals and lots of maturing. Through the people there she learned to be comfortable with herself, accept her limitations and discover her special talents. Easter Seals contributed a lot to making Kay feel good about herself.

Kay also acquired a number of job skills through the Easter Seal program. She went through a whole round of broad-based training, which included sewing and shop work and a variety of activities to see what she was best at and what she liked best.

In addition, the program offered supportive employment and job coaching (where a coach goes to work with an Easter Seal program participant until that participant has mastered all the tasks of of the job). Kay also attended classes there on topics such as personal health and sexual identity.

For a while Kay worked at the center doing fabric cutting but found she was capable of more than that. She's a natural caregiver and since high school has worked part-time at Eagles Manor, a home for the elderly, where she still works two days a week.

Kay then learned sign language and began volunteering at a home for vision- and hearing-impaired children, most of whom also have other multiple disabilities. She loves it there and doesn't mind the feeding tubes and dirty diapers. She just loves the children and is hoping she will be able to get a job there.

Not everybody can do this kind of work, but Kay can and is very good at it, very kind, patient and understanding. Her biggest wish right now is to get an actual job there instead of only being a volunteer.

The other two days of the week Kay does cleaning as part of a mobile maintenance services unit run under the auspices of Easter Seals. She and the others are picked up in a van and taken to various job sites.

The Easter Seal program really helped Kay get the job skills and the daily living skills she needed. Work comes first for Kay now. She has excellent job skills and hates to miss a day of work—even when she's out doing things as the Easter Seal Adult Representative! Easter Seals taught Kay how to help others without doing it for them—an important skill for anyone to have.

Easter Seals also helped me accept Kay's ability to live independently, including living alone in her own apartment. The communication with the Easter Seal people has always been nice and open. Not only did they pay attention to Kay and her needs, they paid attention to me as a parent, and helped me with what I needed to learn about being Kay's mother.

I don't know where we would be without Easter Seals.

## Kay Stewart, 1990 Adult Representative from Great Falls, Montana:

Easter Seals taught me a lot of things—how to write checks, how to take care of my money and how to set little goals for myself whenever I had to get something done. Easter Seals also gave me a lot of training, in the shop and in other areas. The people there even helped me fill out my application for volunteer work at the children's home where I now volunteer and hope I can be hired to be an aide.

I really love those children at the home. They have a lot of needs, but that's all right with me. I play with them as much as I can, and try to teach them little things, like how to press a key on a keyboard and how to press the buttons on a phone. It's my favorite job.

I'm really enjoying being an Adult Representative for Easter seals. It's a lot of fun.

1990 Adult Representative Kay Stewart, mildly mentally disabled.

*Cyndee Pearson is the 1991 National Easter Seal Adult Representative from Vancouver, Washington. She had polio as a child, and today she's an active member of Easter Seals' post-polio support groups.*

## Cyndee Pearson:

*This is a wonderful year to be the Adult Representative. We were all in Chicago at national meetings when the Americans with Disabilities Act passed in the House of Representatives. As an adult with a disability, it meant a great deal to me.*

*I look forward to the opportunities I will have this year to speak about what a difference it makes to have employment and access to our communities. Of course, I'll talk about how Safeway Inc. encouraged me to design the accommodations I would need to work as a pharmacist's assistant. And I'll tell people how different my life is now that I've returned to work and learned to pace myself at home with my family and in my community. People with disabilities do have a lot to offer.*

*1991 National Easter Seal Adult Representative Cyndee Pearson, post-polio syndrome.*

# IX
# White House Visits

*T*hroughout this century our nation's presidents have shown concern for the well-being of the nation's youngest citizens. In 1909 President Theodore Roosevelt convened the first White House Conference on Children. This conference generated new thinking about possible governmental assistance to children with disabilities and, when thousands of veterans of World War I returned home with disabilities incurred in battle, this thinking was extended to include adults with disabilities. As a result of a newly awakened consciousness about the needs of people with disabilities, in 1920 Congress passed the first federal legislation geared to assisting disabled people—the Vocational Rehabilitation Act.

President Hoover's White House conference in 1930 continued looking at the needs of children with disabilities, and many of its ideas formed the basis of the provisions for disabled children in the Social Security Act of 1935.

It seems only fitting then that each National Child since 1953 has been invited to the White House. As any child would, these kids have found the visits among the most memorable moments of their year as National Easter Seal Child. The faces of the presidents in the photos show a warmth of expression and a twinkle in the eyes as they gaze smilingly at the young people who are such an important part of the country they serve.

Of course, as telethon host these last ten years, I have made most of the trips to the Oval Office with the kids and their families. I'll never forget little Shawn Dennsteadt, born without hands, doing a headstand on his skateboard, then flipping off and saying brightly to President Reagan, "Okay, it's your turn!" We all howled, and the President, never at a loss for words, said, "Son, when you get to be my age, you try not to do that anymore."

And another time, when I accompanied Jamie Brazzell, he sang a song his mother had written for him, "Will There Be Ponies In Heaven?" We later asked Jamie and his mom to sing the song on the telethon.

*President Eisenhower in 1955 with National Child Billy Jennings.*

*Mamie Eisenhower in 1953 receiving the year's Easter
Seals from National Child Freddie Wilson, the first
National Child to officially visit the White House.*

*President Eisenhower in 1956 with National Child*
*Clara Jo Proudfoot.* (UPI telephoto)

*Vice-President Richard M. Nixon in 1958 with Mary*
*Lynne Dunnuck.* (UPI telephoto)

*Former president Harry Truman in 1960 receiving a
76th birthday gift from Easter Seal children who sang to
him. (UPI telephoto)*

*President John F. Kennedy in 1961 with Easter Seal*
*National Children Patricia Webber* (left) *and her twin*
*sister Paula and Art Linkletter.* (AP photo)

*President Kennedy with Hedda Hopper and Brenda Heaton. (UPI)*

*Bob Hope and J.P.W. Brown, president of the Easter Seal Society in 1964, watch the antics of National Children, twins Ronnie and Donnie Cooper. (AP wirephoto)*

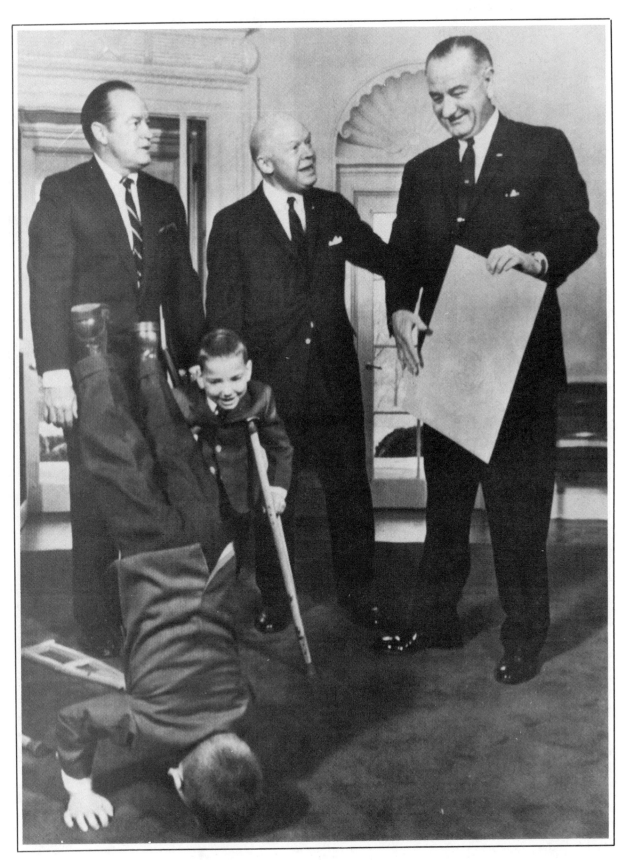

*Jimmy Durante and 1966 National Child Alan Ngao*
*present President Johnson with a sheet of Easter Seals.*

Dinah Shore meets with President Johnson and the 1968
National Children, twins Lisa and Lori Yauch.

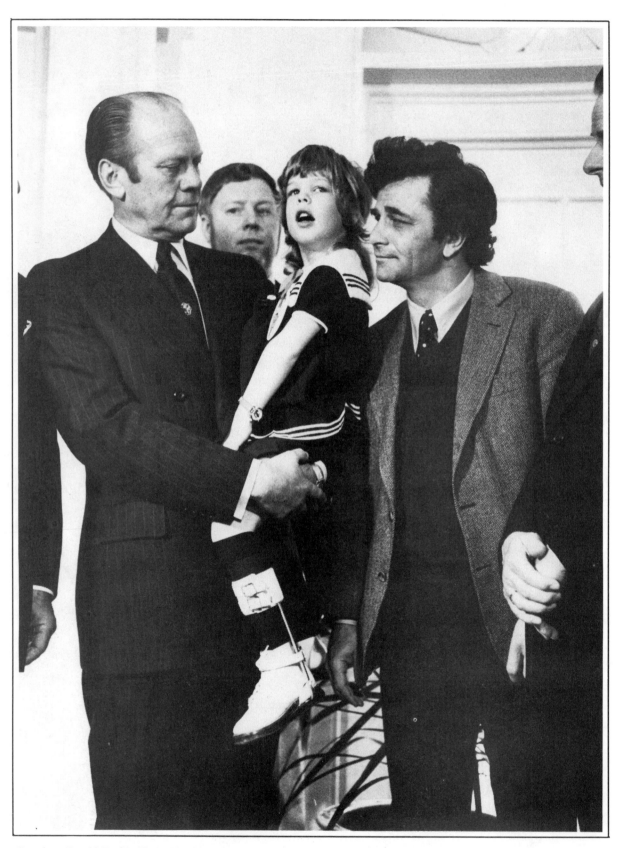

*President Gerald Ford holds 1975 National Child Pamela Jo Baker with Peter Falk at right.*

*First Lady Betty Ford greets a National Easter Seal Child in Hawaii in 1975.* (AP wirephoto)

*President Jimmy Carter chats with 1979 National Child Claire Huckel.* (Photo by Bud Gray)

*President Carter and 1980 National Child Jeanette Alvarado.*

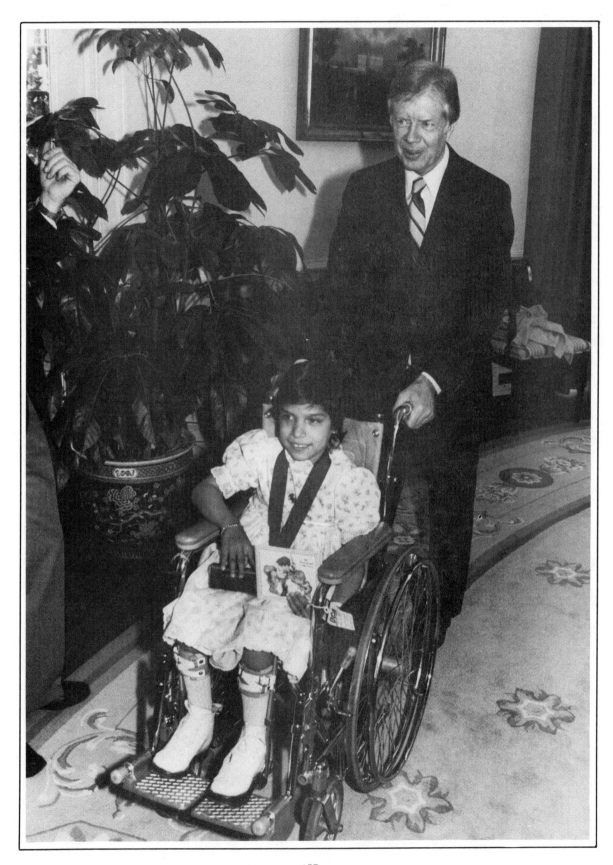

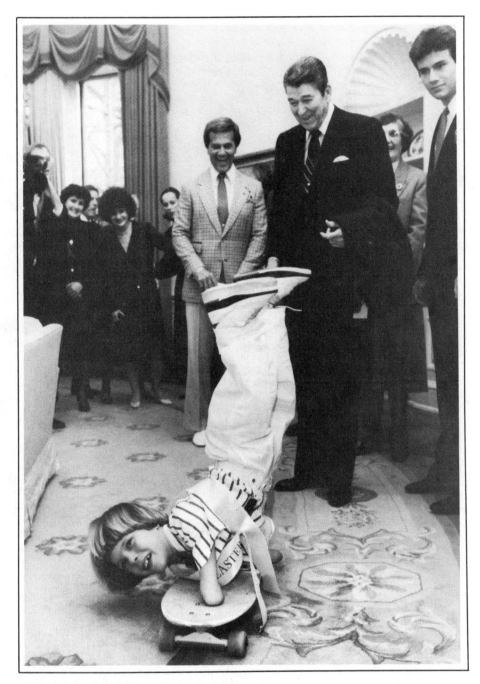

*1988 National Child Shawn Dennsteadt shows President Reagan his skateboarding skills.*

*President and Mrs. Reagan welcome Jamie Brazzell and his family to the White House in 1986.*

*President George Bush welcomes 1989 National Child Joy Hall to the Oval Office.*

*Pat Boone receiving check from Century 21 Real Estate
President Dick Loughlin in 1985 at the telethon.*

# X

# Easter Seal Corporate Sponsors

*F*rom Sidney Albert Gregg, *The Rotarian*, October 1922:

> *This is a business man's movement and is led by Edgar F. Allen, who retired a number of years ago so he could devote his entire time to the erection of a hospital.*

So much has happened in the 71 years of Easter Seals that it's almost easy to forget that the organization did indeed begin as a businessman's movement.

Too often, I feel television and movies and literature, and even the media, malign the business community and project the average successful businessman as uncaring, totally materialistic and focused almost obscenely on the bottom line. This is usually wrong precisely because most successful businessmen also have families, children and grandchildren, and often serious problems and challenges in their personal lives that make them sensitive to others. If that weren't true, there would be no Easter Seals today.

Daddy Allen applied the same sense of vision, drive, guts and organization to the formation of the society as he did to the founding of his own business. In enlisting the help of hundreds of Rotary Clubs across the nation, Allen also tapped into a network of other business people who understood how to get a job done as well he did and how to make things work. Without the help of Rotary, the society would not have survived.

The growth of corporate sponsorship in recent years, then, seems especially fitting, since people in business played such a big part in getting the society going at the start.

Over the years many different corporations have contributed to Easter Seals, each in its own way. In true entrepreneurial fashion, it has encouraged businesses, both large and small, to come up with their own ways to pitch in and help the Easter Seal effort.

Some corporations offer support through Easter Seal product promotion coupons in Sunday newspapers. Some seek contributions from customers, employees, or both. When individual franchises comprise a corporation, as with Century 21 and Amway, each franchise decides if and how to raise money for Easter Seals.

Many corporations hold fund-raising events such as fashion shows, bowling tournaments, car washes, golf tournaments, bike-a-thons, rock-a-thons, dance-a-thons, pie-eating contests and mud-wrestling competitions. Safeway even staged a "sit-a-thon" in Washington, in which people sat in a stadium and raised money according to how long they sat! And they raised tens of thousands of dollars!

There seems to be no limit to the creative ideas people keep coming up with for their Easter Seal fund raisers—ideas that often come from the corporate employees themselves. These fund raisers give people a chance to have a good time while also contributing to a good cause. I host several Easter Seal golf tournaments each year on that very principle!

And what has happened, again and again, is that corporate involvement with Easter Seals has in many cases evolved into something deeper than simply raising much needed funds. It has frequently grown into a commitment to people with disabilities, felt by employees at all levels of the company, from line workers in factories to chief executives in plush offices.

The personal commitments, the personal relationships that have developed between corporate employees and Easter Seals have spurred corporations to increase their hiring of people with disabilities and to assist with advocacy efforts at the community level. Corporate officers have begun serving on Easter Seal boards at the national and local levels. Some corporate executives have even come up with out-of-pocket cash to underwrite public education materials. And many have begun working for changes on their own that will enable people with disabilities to live more independent, fulfilling lives, in a more humane society.

The concept of corporate involvement and ongoing commitment to a cause, termed Social Responsibility Marketing,™ has begun to replace one-time donations of corporate gifts to different charities.

This principle makes such good sense that Easter Seals has encouraged corporate executives to explore the concept. Happily, more and more big companies and their executives are seeing the advantages and practicality of this idea.

With Social Responsibility Marketing,™ a corporation is encouraged to go beyond one-time promotions or gifts. Through education and one-on-one relationships with Easter Seal representatives and clients, corporate sponsors take the next steps, adding new dimensions to their support. This can be through volunteering, hiring people with disabilities, making workplaces accessible or through advocacy efforts, and underwriting the costs of national public education campaigns with Easter Seals.

A large percentage of the funds raised by corporations for Easter Seals come through special events that are run by and involve employees. And that's very appropriate, because corporate sponsorship often reflects the grass roots genius of Easter Seals—the simple concept of people helping people within their own communities.

# Corporate Sponsors Comment

I've asked some of our biggest corporate sponsors to talk about their involvement with Easter Seals. Here's what they have to say.

Nan Van Andel, vice president, communications, Amway Corporation, and chairman of the Amway Easter Seal campaign:

*Besides being a well-known and respected national agency, Easter Seals has local chapters. This enables Amway distributors to put donations to work in their own communities. Both Amway and Easter Seals emphasize service to individuals.*

*Amway Corporation, its employees and independent distributors all contribute to Easter Seals. The corporation contributes directly to the National Easter Seal Society. Amway employees sponsor bowl-a-thons, sporting events and sell special buttons to raise funds. Distributors also host a variety of fund raisers from bowl-a-thons to duck races. They also make direct con-*

*Print ad by Leo Burnett used in 1975 ad campaign.*

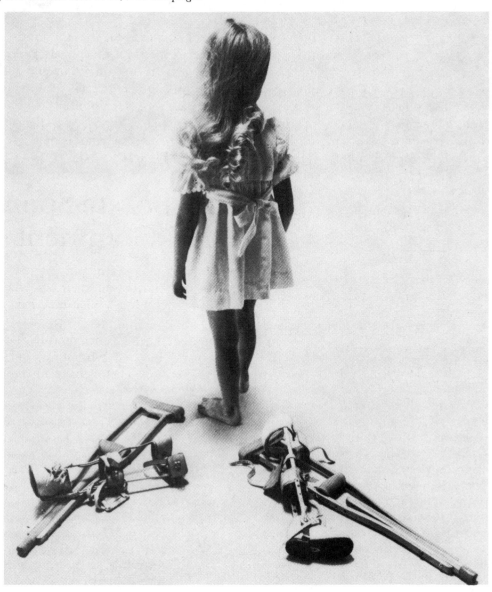

Nan Van Andel, vice president at Amway, (center) and
Patsy Houlihan (left) visit Bridget Houlihan at Easter
Seals' Rocky Mountain Village camp.

tributions and volunteer for their local Easter Seal
societies.

Amway Corporation directs these activities by setting the campaign strategy, suggesting fund-raising
events, creating written and video promotional materials and in general encouraging distributors through
letters and incentives. Amway annually sponsors contests for distributors who raise money for Easter Seals,
awarding ten all-expense paid weekends to Los
Angeles to meet National Easter Seal Society dignitar-
ies and attend the national telethon.

Easter Seal sponsorship has made Amway people
more aware of the needs of the world at large and
has helped employees and distributors gain a better
understanding of people with disabilities. Our sponsorship joins everyone at Amway together in a common
goal for a worthwhile cause.

Dick Loughlin, Chief Executive Officer,
Century 21 Real Estate Corporation:

Our involvement with Easter Seals began in 1979
when a group of brokers approached our international
headquarters with the idea of giving something back
to the communities in which they worked. After looking into several charities Easter Seals seemed the natural choice. We were impressed that Easter Seals used
such a large percentage of its funds to provide direct
services to people with disabilities and such a low percentage for fund raising, management, and general
expenses. Century 21 brokers and sales associates especially liked the fact that the money they raised for
Easter Seals would be used within their own community for services and programs.

*Century 21 International's top award-winning float in the 1990 Tournament of Roses Parade featured 1990 National Easter Seal Child Vanessa Vance.*

*Century 21 has been the largest corporate sponsor of Easter Seals, raising over $25 million in contributions between 1979 and 1990, even though, as an individually owned franchise organization, participation in Easter Seal fund raising is totally voluntary. Our brokers, sales associates and regional offices generate donations by organizing an endless variety of fund-raising projects each year, from bake sales to dinner dances to auctions. Many events have become local traditions in their communities. Several brokers now even build houses and donate the net proceeds to their local Easter Seal societies.*

*Our involvement with Easter Seals has been a relationship builder. The fund-raising events have provided our co-workers with feelings of unity, warmth and camaraderie. Participating offices benefit from increased name recognition and enhanced image within their communities.*

*Easter Seals has given us a common cause and the pride of giving to our communities.*

Bob Bradford, senior vice president, Safeway Stores, Inc.:

*Safeway's affiliation with Easter Seals is one of the best corporate decisions we have ever made. The warm feeling of accomplishment that Safeway employees have in helping Easter Seals help others has become the best morale booster in our company. Easter Seals and Safeway is a real love story.*

*Safeway's A&W Root Beer float sales alone raised $330,000 for Easter Seals in 1989.*

*1990 Easter Seal Child Vanessa Vance with Eugene Freedman and the Enesco cheerleaders during her visit to the Easter Seal Kick-off Rally at Enesco Corporate Headquarters.*

Gene Freedman, president and chief executive officer, Enesco Corporation:

*We're proud to identify with a loving, caring, sharing organization like Easter Seals. Through our involvement with the telethon and everything related to it, I feel that we have become a better company. Being identified as a national sponsor makes us very proud, and I want to thank Easter Seals for helping our company achieve success.*

167

*A Friendly Restaurants employee prepares for a "Cones for Kids" Easter Seal fund-raising event.*

# National Easter Seal Society Corporate Sponsors (1990)

A & W Beverages, Inc.
American Airlines
Amway Corporation
CENTURY 21 Real Estate
    Corporation

Comprehensive Accounting Corporation
Eddie Bauer, Inc.
Ekco Housewares, Inc.
Enesco Corporation
Epsilon Sigma Alpha
    International
Fraternal Order of Police/
    Associates/Auxiliary
Friendly Ice Cream Corporation
International Brotherhood
    of Teamsters
Little Caesar Enterprises
Mattel, Inc.

*1986 National Easter Seal Child Jamie Brazzell and Pat Boone visit with a Safeway driver.*

National Snowmobile
    Foundation
Rotary International
Safeway Stores, Inc.
Toys "R" Us, Inc.
Uniglobe Travel
    International, Inc.

# FSI Coupon Sponsors (1990)

First Mail Information
Florida Citrus Commission
Glenbrook Laboratories
The Kellogg Company
Nestlé Foods Corporation

# XI
# Celebrities: Their Finest Hours

*D*addy's memoirs:

*During the early days of 1922 [we] ... decided ... to bring out a film depicting the entire work of crippled children and its connection with Rotary. This arrangement was made and carried through by James Bateman of Cleveland, then Executive Secretary of International.*

*It took quite a good many months to prepare the picture and we had to have a great many different interested people to be used as film artists, and I must say that as a whole it was a very commendable piece of work ....*

*It started with the finding by a Rotarian of a little crippled girl in a rather tumbled down home and it followed that little girl to a clinic, to a hospital and the return of that child to the mother, throwing away the crutches.*

*In the final scene hundreds and hundreds of Rotarians [are] marching over the world showing the world development of help to millions of children as had been given to this one child.*

*This picture was finished in the fall of 1922.*

In the very first years of the society, and even in the early days of film itself, Daddy Allen had a movie made to inform people about the growing movement toward helping people with disabilities.

He understood that the success of this movement depended upon people knowing about it. He also understood the importance of the visual image in communicating an idea.

Movies, photographs, television and videotapes—all means of presenting visual images—have contributed significantly to the work and growth of Easter Seals. The images show people what Easter Seals is all about—who gets services, who gives them, what the services look like and where the services are provided. They also remind people that the money they donate to Easter Seals goes to help real people, individuals with names and faces, rather than to some abstract organization.

Since the first National Child in 1947, the society's visual images have also included a number of celebrities—from radio, television, movies, sports, politics, the arts—photographed or filmed with many different Easter Seal children.

The celebrities have enjoyed meeting the children and their parents, and gained satisfaction from lending their names to a cause they wanted to support and draw attention to. And the kids—well, what child wouldn't want to meet his or her favorite movie or television star!

The celebrities who have promoted the work of Easter Seals over the decades now comprise a long and impressive list. Some of the best-loved people from many fields, a great many no longer with us, expressed a real commitment through their help during the campaigns. Though most of them have trophies and awards and every kind of industry recognition, I think they'd agree with me that their work for Easter Seals is among their finest and most significant.

*Peter Falk with Rachel Rosenberg in 1975.*

*Meadowlark Lemon of the Harlem Globetrotters with
National Easter Seal Child Randy Wright in 1973.*

*Lucille Ball serving ice cream to Easter Seal children.*

*Carol Burnett with National Child Jo Ann Schaffer in 1971.*

*Hank Aaron of the Atlanta Braves pins an Easter Seal button on National Child Tammy Bryant in 1974.*

*Telethon co-host Mike Douglas in 1975 with National
Child Pammie Jo Baker.*

# XII
# The Telethon

*T*he telethon is really all I knew about Easter Seals before I made my commitment, and I didn't know much about that. Besides, as you already know, I was prepared not to get involved.

I was sure it would be long and tiring to host a telethon, virtually thankless after a couple of days, and I'd be drained for weeks.

I was right and wrong. It was long and tiring, that first year especially—but it certainly wasn't thankless, and it was so exhilarating that I almost felt guilty when people were thanking me for weeks after. It was one of the more exciting and fulfilling adventures of my entire life and career.

I love the power of telethons to mobilize in people, and what they seem to galvanize. They bring out the best in folks, cause them to focus on the needs and concerns of others and prompt them to find ways to reach out and help. It's an amazing and largely American phenomenon.

They do much more than entertain. They show what Easter Seals is, what it does and give people a chance to be involved, to take part in something really important, to change things, to make a difference in the lives of others.

Telethons are just the tip of the iceberg, of course, as far as Easter Seals is concerned. But that very visible tip attracts the attention and the active involvement of millions of people, and helps the whole institution to carry on its activities all year long.

Really, telethons are the modern version of Daddy Allen's visits to Rotary Clubs all over the country. They inform people, and bring people together in a very unique way.

They create a tapestry of neighbors helping neighbors. You might not realize it (though I say it over and over again), but more than 90 percent of the dollars raised in each year's telethon stays in the same state, and likely in the same community, from which the donations originates. That means when you call and pledge to Easter Seals, your contribution is going directly to help your own friends and neighbors.

Telethons seem to bring out the best instincts in everybody. Maybe it's because they're marathons—and somebody is going to extraordinary lengths to set a record. The viewers get involved and want the fundraising to succeed. They want to see those people achieve their goal, and they want to be part of it too.

Telethons nudge people out of themselves and help them focus for awhile on something larger than their own concerns. Very important, they provide an outlet for people's natural instinct to want to give and to be helpful to others.

We've always taken the high road with Easter Seal telethons, accentuating the positive. We show what people with disabilities can do. We're not there to stir up pity, or play on guilt or obligation. We're there to bring out the best in people. Our telethons show how much people with disabilities are capable of.

When they are seen by 60 million or more people over a 20-hour period, they really can accomplish a lot.

Among other things, telethons reach people who need Easter Seal services but who might not know what these services are and where they are available.

Telethons, of course, raise money for therapy and other services for people with disabilities. If telethon revenues decreased, Easter Seals would have to cut direct services. This would be felt by the people who need those services most—the child with a serious disability who wants to go to summer camp, the young girl who needs therapy for a spinal cord injury, the adult with cerebral palsy who needs a computer so he or she can work and make a living.

Easter Seals aired its first telethon in 1972. Each year the telethon has received increased support from the public, volunteers and corporate sponsors. And each year—as a direct result—the number of people Easter Seals has been able to help has also grown.

Telethons provide a way for people to impart the "Power to Overcome."

And what a logical outgrowth of that tiny little Easter Seal stamp itself! For as Daddy Allen knew, and A.H. Thompson of the Kentucky Society in 1934 expressed, "The penny seal" (and I can add the 20-hour vast network telethon) "is the finest method in the world of telling your story and winning friends in a cause like ours, because it gives everyone a chance, from the newsboy to the millionaire, to make his contribution. And once having given he will never forget he's helping crippled children."

And though we never use the phrase "crippled children" anymore, the principle is right on target, and almost divine in its profundity.

# XIII
# The Dream Gets
# Better All the Time

*T*he story is so big, but the pictures tell the story as well or better than words. They should inspire you to think about ways you can get involved in this magnificent undertaking. If you haven't watched the telethon and contributed—look for it in the early spring (there'll be plenty of publicity in *TV Guide* and the newspapers) and experience the genuine thrill of picking up the phone and calling in a pledge, and then honoring that pledge with a check. Whether large or small, or somewhere in between, you'll know that you're a part of this ongoing saga, and that you are helping admirable and deserving people right around you.

In fact, ask around, check the phone book and hospitals if necessary and visit an Easter Seal facility. See for yourself what some of your neighbors are doing through volunteer efforts to improve the quality of life of people with disabilities. If you're interested, the center will probably have something for you to do.

You will find that it will mean a great deal to your neighbors with disabilities, but it will also do you a lot of good. Listen to these last words from Daddy Allen at the International Convention in 1930:

*. . . [A]ll human endeavor has its spiritual side and all human endeavor relates itself to the spirit of the individual. There is a real compensation always, whether it be sought or not to those who . . . strive to assist their less fortunate fellow men. . . .*

*Remaking the body is a noble undertaking . . . but the re-creation of the spirit is the crowning act of all endeavors. . . .*

*Let all who are interested understand and feel that behind us and above us is intelligence and love. As doubters we will not achieve. As skeptics we will not contribute. As cynics we will not create.*

*Faith is the great motive power and no organization will realize its full possibilities unless its members have a deep conviction that life is important and that their work well done becomes part of an unending plan.*

As usual, it's difficult to add much to what Daddy Allen said himself. After all, this was his dream, and nobody saw it more clearly or could articulate its principles better than he could.

I wish I could have known him. Doing the research for this book, I feel I have come to know him, at least in spirit and in practice and in practical application of energies and altruism. But I'd really like to have heard his voice, felt some of the excitement he must have exuded, seen how he reconciled the heavy demands of his marvelous work with his home life and his relationship with his wife. She must have been a remarkable woman too.

And finally, I would love to have asked them, as a couple, how their work for children with disabilities helped them in adjusting to the loss of their son and reconciling it. As tragic and unacceptable as that must have been, I expect they'd tell me that only that kind of trauma would have redirected their lives and priorities toward helping people with disabilities.

They planted a seed, a costly seed, a precious treasure, and a mighty tree eventually grew in its place.

Remember that spring is the season for celebrations of rebirth. And this is what Easter Seal programs and services set out to provide—the chance for children and adults with disabilities to achieve independenc in this society—a new and better quality of life.

So there are, I truly believe, echoes of nature in this whole Easter Seal enterprise. There is something in each of us that wants to give, to help and encourage others. There is a part of each of us that wants to cheer a worthy and striving competitor across the finish line to victory.

We want to make a difference, we desire to participate in things that really matter, it thrills us to change things for the better somehow. And most of us want the chance to share our blessings with others. Personally, I think we're just made that way.

Aren't most of us really willing, perhaps eager, to help others if someone will organize the work and show us how?

Daddy Allen knew this or discovered it as he went along. As well as anyone I've heard about in our day, he knew how to tap into this well, this reservoir of human kindness. Good intentions alone aren't enough; there really has to be a practical understanding of the many ways that we can help to achieve the goals, and at the same time an empathy for others our efforts will benefit. And above all, perhaps, there needs to be a willingness to match conviction with elbow grease, lots of sacrificial effort and action.

And it must not hurt to be persuasive and charismatic.

Daddy Allen was all of this, and my hat's off to the man, and to his wife, because she must have been a major source of support and encouragement to him. What a thrill it had to be, for both of them, to see what grew from that early desire to build a small new hospital in Elyria, Ohio, to help their neighbors.

And though he was certainly a man of immense vision, I doubt that even Daddy Allen imagined the vast scope and effectiveness of the Easter Seal program today, after its first 71 years.

Daddy Allen, my friend and inspiration, the best is yet to come. Thanks for showing us and exemplifying the human touch.

# Appendix

## Chronology

1919  Ohio Society for Crippled Children formed in Elyria, Ohio.

1920  Passage of the Federal Vocational Rehabilitation Act, a limited program not expanded for more than 20 years.

1921  National Society for Crippled Children formed in Elyria, Ohio, the only national voluntary agency speaking and acting on behalf of children with disabilities. Until then no concerted effort existed for treatment and rehabilitation of people with disabilities by either public or voluntary agencies. Only a few state tax-supported programs existed, and federal-state programs for children with disabilities were not enacted until almost a decade later.

1922  National Society for Crippled Children becomes the International Society for Crippled Children, maintaining function as a national agency, with state affiliates, as well as affiliation with voluntary societies in other countries.

Affiliated societies form in Michigan and New York.

The Rotary International Convention approves a "resolution to develop interest in work on behalf of crippled children."

1923  Affiliated societies form in Illinois, Kentucky, Pennsylvania, Tennessee and West Virginia.

1924  National society opens a Bureau of Information and Library.

1929  First World Congress for Welfare of Cripples held in Geneva, Switzerland.

Twenty-three states have formed state Societies for Crippled Children

1930  National society supplies basic data for White House Conference on Child Health and Protection. President Hoover meets with 3,000 medical, educational and social experts to "study the present status of the health and well-being of the children of the United States; to report what is being done; to recommend what ought to be done and how to do it." The Committee on the Physically and Mentally Handicapped develops a Bill of Rights for the Handicapped Child.

1934  The first Easter seals issued as fund-raising device. Eight state societies participate and the entire campaign raised $47,000.

1935  Passage of the first Social Security

Act. The national society and its affiliates have worked hard for Title V of this act, which provides an annual appropriation to states that submit approved plans for "services for locating crippled children and for providing medical, surgical, corrective and other services and care, and facilities for diagnosis, hospitalization and after care for children who are crippled or who are suffering from conditions that lead to crippling."

1937　By April 1, 42 states, Alaska, Hawaii and the District of Columbia have submitted approved plans for services to children with disabilities under provisions of the Social Security Act.

Easter Seal Society supports a bill proposing federal appropriations to states to assist in educating children with all types of physically disabling conditions.

1939　Easter Seals is a founding member of the International Society for the Welfare of Cripples, known since 1969 as Rehabilitation International.

The International Society for Crippled Children separates into different organizations—the International Society for the Welfare of Cripples (now known as the International Society for Rehabilitation of the Disabled) and the National Society for Crippled Children of the United States of America (now known as the National Easter Seal Society.)

1940　First issue of *Bulletin on Current Literature* (predecessor to *Rehabilitation Literature*) for professionals in field of disabilities.

1941　Society is founding member of National Association of Sheltered Workshops and Homebound Programs.

1944　Society changes its name to the National Society for Crippled Children and Adults, adding "Adults" and

dropping "of the United States of America."

1945　Society reorganizes and moves its headquarters to Chicago. An era of expansion follows.

Society establishes the first network of Cerebral Palsy Treatment Centers in the United States.

Forty states have societies in various stages of development.

1947　First National Easter Seal Child named—15-year-old Harold Ferrell of Redwood City, California.

Society is founding member of the American Academy for Cerebral Palsy.

1950　Society attains affiliates in every state, the District of Columbia and Puerto Rico.

Society is founding member of the American Psychological Association's Division 22 (Psychological Aspects of Disability) and of the National Committee for Research in Neurological and Communicative Disorders.

1952　Society adopts the stylized lily as its symbol (and later, its trademark). The Societies for Children and Adults with Disabilities are informally referred to as "the Easter Seal Societies."

Society is founding member of the Association of Rehabilitation Centers, previously known as the Conference of Rehabilitation Centers.

1953　Establishment of the Easter Seal Research Foundation, meeting the third major objective of the society, in addition to direct services and educational programs.

1955　President Eisenhower becomes the first president to help launch that year's annual Easter Seal campaign.

The national society co-sponsors an Exposition on the Employment of the Handicapped Worker, which presented a cross-section of industries in which workers with disabilities could perform a variety of tasks.

1956 The Easter Seal Research Foundation awards its first grants to support applied and basic research on disabling conditions and rehabilitation.

1958 The national society initiates a project with the President's Committee on the Employment of the Handicapped on the development of an American standard that would make buildings accessible and useable by people with disabilities.

The national society built and occupied its own building in the West Side Medical Center in Chicago.

1959 The first issue of *Rehabilitation Literature*, a professional journal on rehabilitation, is published.

1960 The society initiates a pilot study on minimal brain dysfunction and conducts the first research on this subject.

1960 The society hosts the eighth ISRD World Congress in New York with 4,000 delegates from 80 nations.

1960 The society launches a national campaign on elimination of architectural barriers.

1961 Completion of standards to make buildings accessible was announced at the Easter Seal Annual Convention. Approved by the American National Standards Institute, the standards resulted from a research project at the University of Illinois under a grant from the Easter Seal Research Foundation. The standards became part of PL 90-480, which insured that "certain buildings financed with federal funds are so designed and constructed as to be accessible to the physically handicapped." Easter Seals then begins a nationwide educational and acting campaign to eliminate architectural barriers in all buildings used by the public.

1963 A Massachusetts Institute of Technology self-study brings sweeping re-organization of Easter Seals.

1964 Easter Seals is recognized by the President's Committee on Employment of the Handicapped for its leadership role in removing architectural barriers.

1967 The society incorporates the words "Easter Seal" into its official title in a name change that acknowledges the association of the general public with the organization's traditional campaign symbol.

1969 On the recommendation of the National Health Council, Easter Seals is selected to represent voluntary health organizations on the President's National Center for Voluntary Action. Easter Seals' executive director chairs the task force on immunization against rubella, a project of the center.

1971 First Easter Seal Telethon beamed from Las Vegas, hosted by Monty Hall.

1972 The society mandates that all Easter Seal rehabilitation facilities be accredited by the Commission on Accreditation of Rehabilitation Facilities by 1977.

1973 The society assisted in the passage of the Rehabilitation Act of 1973, which for the first time recognized civil rights of people with disabilities.

1974 Board of directors adopts Easter Seal position encouraging advocacy efforts on behalf of persons with disabilities.

1975 First National Barrier Awareness Week sponsored by Easter Seals to focus public attention on the elimination of environmental and attitudinal barriers and emphasizing abilities of people with disabilities.

The society assisted in the development of the Education for All Handicapped Children's Act (P.L. 94-142).

1977  The society planned and participated in the White House Conference on Handicapped Individuals.

1979  Elimination of the phrase "for Crippled Children and Adults" from the National Easter Seal Society name because the term "crippled" has a negative connotation to people with disabilities and was no longer acceptable in the rehabilitation field.

Highly successful management training for Easter Seal administrators initiated in conjunction with major universities, i.e., Harvard, Stanford.

1980  Initiated a national accessibility/advocacy program with presentations to over 50 conventions and meetings of professional and trade groups.

Provided lead role in passage of legislation expanding Medicare coverage to all services provided by comprehensive outpatient rehabilitation facilities.

1981  The society led efforts that provided appropriations of $2 million annually for recreation projects for people with disabilities.

1982  The society served 759,000 individuals, a record number of people benefitting from Easter Seal services.

Program expenditures reached an all-time high of $111.6 million.

Broadened representation on the Easter Seal Research Foundation and scope to include applied research.

Conduct first manufacturers' coupon fund-raising program.

1983  Cumulative telethon totals surpassed $100 million mark.

Began development of management information systems to make computer training, software and hardware available to affiliates.

1984  In fiscal 1983–84 Easter Seal services serve a record one million-plus people.

The Voting Accessibility for the Elderly and Handicapped Act is signed into law by President Reagan after intensive lobbying efforts by the National Easter Seal Society and its affiliates.

All affiliates adopt a common identity that includes the words Easter Seal in their names.

1985  Easter Seal Professional Advisory Council report, "Health Care in Transition," identifies and interprets major trends affecting delivery of rehabilitation services.

Easter Seal affiliates become indirectly involved in research sponsored through the Easter Seal Research Foundation.

Marketing and sales program launched for Easter Seal Systems' line of customized computer software and consulting services

Legislative Action Nework established to directly involve affiliates in mobilizing grass roots support for Easter Seal advocacy efforts.

1986  Easter Seals continues to serve over one million people, 40 percent of whom are adults.

National society launches attitudes campaign to educate the public about the dignity and potential of persons with disabilities to dispel myths and stereotypes.

Easter Seal Systems introduces new Medical Rehabilitation Manager Software System and co-sponsors program evaluation and automation workshops with other national health care organizations.

Easter Seals plays active role in independent sector's fight to preserve the personal income tax deduction for charitable contributions.

Easter Seals plays leadership role in Alliance of Nonprofit Mailers' efforts to prevent further postal rate increases for nonprofit organizations.

1987    Easter Seals is recognized by the National Health Council as the nationwide leader among voluntary, nonprofit healthcare organizations for the percentage of program dollars spent on direct client services—93 percent. *Program Digest*, a new quarterly review, is launched to provide state and local societies with a vehicle for monitoring the latest in program management concerns.

Easter Seal advocacy efforts play key role in passage of the Air Carrier Access Act of 1986; the Rehabilitation Act Amendments of 1986; the Education of the Handicapped Amendments of 1986; and the enactment of tax provisions authorizing deductions for barrier removal and work expenses for persons with disabilities who have special needs; funding for health and rehabilitation programs; the Fair Labor Standard Act Amendments.

Easter Seals commissions the production of a Second City-style of comedy revue about people with disabilities entitled "Doin' the Reality Rag."

Easter Seal Systems introduces Rehabware, the world's only totally integrated computer software designed to meet the needs of vocational and medical rehabilitation facilities.

1988    Easter Seals serves over one million people for the fourth consecutive year.

National Health Council once again cities Easter Seals as nationwide leader among voluntary health organizations for 93 percent of its program dollars being spent on direct services.

Congress appropriates $1 million for the national society to conduct a multiyear project to improve access to mass transportation for people with disabilities.

Model Programs project launched as first phase of National Strategic Program Plan to select develop and implement model programs for use by Easter Seal affiliates.

National Society receives RESNA Leadership Award from the Rehabilitation Engineering Society of North America for "outstanding contribution to the field of rehabilitation technology."

1989    National society launches Project Action, a multi-year project to improve access to mass transportation for people with disabilities with a Congressional appropriation of almost $3 million.

More than 120 Easter Seal Societies participate in Friends Who Care disability awareness public education campaign. Ronald McDonald Children's Charities awards $350,000 for an elementary-school Friends Who Care curriculum development and national distribution.

Easter Seals ends a decade of tremendous growth. From 1980 to 1989:
— Provided services for 9,414,600 children and adults with disabilities and their families.
— Raised $1,867,400,000 to support Easter Seal programs and services. 90 percent of this money was spent in the states where it was raised.

1990    Easter Seals plays a key role in the disability coalition that helped to write and encourage passage of the landmark Americans with Disabilities Act, which guarantees basic civil rights for people with disabilities.

# National Easter Seal Children

| Year | Name | Disability | City |
|------|------|-----------|------|
| 1947 | Harold Ferrell | Cerebral Palsy | Redwood City, California |
| 1948 | Mike Golden | Cerebral Palsy | Denver, Colorado |
| 1949 | Bette Jean Bligh | | Jamestown, North Dakota |
| 1950 | Russell Miller | Cerebral Palsy | Columbus, Ohio |
| 1951 | Brett Downes | Cerebral Palsy | Hampton, Virginia |
| 1952 | Doris Desrosiers | Cerebral Palsy | Nashau, New Hampshire |
| 1953 | Freddie Wilson | Spastic Quadriplegia | Reno, Nevada |
| 1954 | Karen Albrecht | Cerebral Palsy | San Antonio, Texas |
| 1955 | Billy Jennings | Paraplegic | Bridgeport, Connecticut |
| 1956 | Clara Jo Proudfoot | Spina bifida | Miami, Florida |
| 1957 | Walter Bill Cash | Polio | Clear Lake, Iowa |
| 1958 | Mary Lynne Dunnuch | Cerebral Palsy | Yuma, Arizona |
| 1959 | Philip Little | | York, Pennsylvania |
| 1960 | John Kemp | Born with arms above elbows, left leg above knee, right leg below knee | Bismarck, North Dakota |
| 1961 | Webber Twins Patricia and Paula | Cerebral Palsy | South Carolina |
| 1962 | Tommy Doyle | Perthes | Manhattan Beach, California |
| 1963 | Brenda Heaton | CP | Downers Grove, Illinois |
| 1964 | The Cooper Twins | Cerebral Palsy | Coal Creek, Colorado |
| 1965 | Barbara Staten | 70% of body burned | Indianapolis, Indiana |
| 1966 | Alan Nagao | Born with right leg ending at thigh | Honolulu, Hawaii |
| 1967 | Leigh Anne Huff | Spinal | Decatur, Georgia |
| 1968 | Lori & Lisa Yauch | Spastic paraplegia | Detroit, Michigan |

| Year | Name | Condition | Location |
|------|------|-----------|----------|
| 1969 | Dona Kay Howell | Rare childhood stroke | Tallahassee, Florida |
| 1970 | Lori Jean Bowen | Spina bifida | Columbus, Ohio |
| 1971 | Peter Jon Heltemes | Cerebral Palsy | Rockville, Maryland |
| 1972 | Jo Ann Schaffer | Cerebral Palsy | Northampton, Pennsylvania |
| 1973 | Peter Stinson | Spina bifida | Sacramento, California |
| 1974 | Tammy Bryant | Brain injury | Albany, Georgia |
| 1975 | Pamela Jo Baker | Cerebral Palsy | Wellsburg, West Virginia |
| 1976 | Kerri Lynn Hines | Cerebral Palsy | Waterford, Michigan |
| 1977 | Danya Steele | Meningomyelocele with stenosis of the spinal cord | Little Rock, Arkansas |
| 1978 | Anthony Zidek | Spina bifida | Wonder Lake, Illinois |
| 1979 | Claire Huckel | Cerebral Palsy | Philadelphia, Pennsylvania |
| 1980 | Jeanette Alvarado | Spina bifida | San Antonio, Texas |
| 1981 | Colleen Finn | Spina bifida | Shelton, Connecticut |
| 1982 | Mary Anne Sacco | Early acquired encephalopathy 2 neonatal subarachnoid hemorrhage with secondary hydrocephalus | Milton, Mass |
| 1983 | Matthew Huston | Transverse myelitis | Glendale, Arizona |
| 1984 | Stephanie Swiney | Spina bifida | Welcome, North Carolina |
| 1985 | Danielle Newman | Spina bifida | Alsip, Illinois |
| 1986 | Jamie Brazzell | Quadriplegic from spinal cord injury | Mayfield, Kentucky |
| 1987 | Susie Wilcox | Spina bifida | West Simsbury, Connecticut |
| 1988 | Shawn Dennsteadt | Femur-fibula-ulna syndrome | Mt. Laurel, New Jersey |
| 1989 | Joy Hall | Cerebral Palsy | Baltimore, Maryland |
| 1990 | Vanessa Vance | Spina bifida | San Antonio, Texas |
| 1991 | Bridget Houlihan | Cerebral Palsy | Denver, Colorado |

# Presidents of the National Easter Seal Society

| | |
|---|---|
| 1921–1934 | Mr. Edgar F. Allen, Elyria, Ohio |
| 1934–1937 | Mr. Edgar F. Allen, President Emeritus |
| 1934–1940 | Mr. Paul H. King |
| 1940–1948 | Col. E. W. Palmer, Kingsport, Tennessee |
| 1948–1949 | Mr. John H. Lee, Ph.D., Michigan |
| 1949–1950 | Mr. William H. Jaenicke, California |
| 1950–1951 | Mr. Gerald M. Ungaro, Chicago |
| 1951–1952 | Mr. Davis E. Geiger, Ashland, Kentucky |
| 1952–1953 | Dr. William T. Sanger, Richmond, Virginia |
| 1953–1954 | Mr. J. Raymond Tiffany, Montclair, New Jersey |
| 1954–1955 | Mr. Edgar Kobak, New York |
| 1955–1957 | Mr. Theodore H. Wegener, Boise, Idaho |
| 1957–1958 | Mr. Paul Dietrich, Los Angeles |
| 1958–1959 | Mr. John H. Lee, Ph.D., Michigan |
| 1959–1961 | Hon. Joseph J. Foss, South Dakota |
| 1961–1962 | Mr. Elwood M. Brooks, Denver, Colorado |
| 1962–1963 | Mr. Carl A. Morring, Jr., Huntsville, Alabama |
| 1963–1965 | Mr. J. P. W. Brown, Tennessee |
| 1965–1967 | Mr. T. A. Mangelsdorf, New Kent, Virginia |
| 1967–1969 | Mr. Leon Chatelain, Jr., Washington, D.C. |
| 1969–1971 | Mr. George A. Haas, Atlanta |
| 1971–1973 | Mr. Thomas C. Teas, Mason City, Iowa |
| 1973–1974 | Mr. A. Clay Stewart, Lexington, Kentucky |
| 1974–1975 | Mr. Edward J. Drake, Dallas |
| 1975–1977 | Mr. Lamar Soutter, M.D., Concord, Massachusetts |
| 1977–1978 | Mr. Charles C. Campbell, Albuquerque, NM |
| 1978–1980 | Mrs. Edward (Johanna) Plaut, New Canaan, Connecticut |
| 1980–1982 | Mrs. Tom (Gloria) Cook, Jr., Ormond Beach, Florida |
| 1983–1984 | Mr. Michael N. Smith, Stockton, California |
| 1985–1986 | Mr. R. B. Coats, Mobile, Alabama |
| 1987–88 | Mrs. Thomas (Elizabeth) Kershaw, Jr., Wakefield, Rhode Island |
| 1989– | Mr. Walter A. Spencer, Jr., Pennsylvania |